Aunt Quimby's
Reminiscences of Georgia

The Reprint Company
Spartanburg, South Carolina

This Volume Was Reproduced
From An 1871 Edition
In The
University of Georgia Libraries
Athens, Georgia

The Reprint Company
Post Office Box 5401
Spartanburg, South Carolina 29301

Reprinted: 1972
ISBN 0-87152-077-X
Library of Congress Catalog Card Number: 74-187382

Manufactured in the United States of America on long-life paper.

Publisher's Note

In the reproduction of century-old books such as *Aunt Quimby's Reminiscences of Georgia,* problems develop at times which, it is hoped, will not interfere with the reader's pleasure at having the rare material available once again.

One of the constant problems is locating original copies clean and clear enough to photograph. This proved to be a major problem in the publication of this reprint edition.

After an extensive search, the only copy located was the one belonging to the University of Georgia in Athens. However, this copy has been laminated for protection. Consequently, the reader will notice some unevenness in the printing from page to page and some of the words may appear blurred.

Also, there are a few pages in the front of the book on which some words have broken letters and some lines of type are broken. Without another copy available, no attempt to restore these words was made.

It is hoped that these discrepancies in this reprint edition will appear slight to the reader. The publisher believes that making the book available again in this form outweighs the disadvantage of having it available only in a rare book collection.

The Reprint Company

AUNT QUIMEY'S

REMINISCENCES

OF GEORGIA.

--BY--

L. R. FEWELL.

MERIDIAN, MISS[illegible]PPI:
[illegible] & [illegible], STEAM PRINTERS, [illegible]HNSON S[illegible],

DEDICATION:

TO the many friends in Georgia whose kindness and attention to the sojourner in their midst can never be forgotton while life lasts, this pamphlet is affectionately dedicated by the author, with the hope that its perusal may serve to while away some otherwise dull hours, especially for [illegible] were the sharers in the excursion herein described, and for the truth of whose incidents they can vouch.

MERIDIAN, April 23d, 1871.

AUNT QUIMBY'S

REIMNISCENCES OF GEORGIA.

CHAPTER I.

"HO FOR THE FALLS!" cried a small, wizen-faced boy, rapping lustily at the door of one of the houses in W——, just as the first rays of the sun began to brighten the cloudless sky of an August morning. "Ho for the Falls!" repeated a portly old bachelor, on the shady side of forty, popping his head out of a window on the opposite side of the street; and the cry was caught up and re-echoed till the whole village was astir. In every house hurried toilets were being made and hasty breakfasts eaten, while swift-footed runners sped from house to house bearing messages and parcels forgotten till the last moment. A general air of bustle and life had replaced the every day sleepiness of the place, which was so small that a very slight excitement would stir up its inhabitants, each of whom, of course, knew all about his neighbors affairs, and was ready at the shortest notice to attend to them. *Now*, those not personally interested were eager to bestow words of advice, approval or warning upon the actors in the affair, which had been more than a nine days talk for their village.

As the morning progressed, the cause of the commotion was visible in the appearance on the public square of a motley assemblage of persons, and a variety of vehicles and horses of almost every size and color. In front was a light buggy drawn by a sprightly colt, whose feet, in this its first drive, had a tendency to fly above its head. This was occupied by the pioneer of the party, whose portly form wrapped in a linen duster bore as little resemblance to the inimitable creation of Cooper's pen—Leatherstocking—as the party he led, the ladies radiant in ruffles and crinoline, the gentlemen in dusters and fashionable hats—to the hardy hunters a pers which that noted character led through so many a We will see if a few weeks among the mountains will so the difference less apparent. for if, as some assert, civil and not nature creates the difference among men, then, s in leaving its bounds, some of the original elements of c ter will be exhibited.

Next in order came a long-bodied, high topped affair, w the pleasure-seekers had tried to dignify with the name of nibus; but, though thoroughly renovated and converted other uses, it still retained its former name of ambulan This striking vehicle was drawn by a pair of horses, if th could be termed a *pair* which was totally unlike in size, shap and color; one, being a tall clay bank or yellowish roan, carry ing such a high head that he seemed to be constantly viewing the sky with his one good eye, or searching among the tree tops for some excuse to take fright, and, by running, relieve the constant excitement of his nervous body; the other, a flea-bitten gray, whose many years of service at the plow had given his head such an earthward tendency that his body followed the example of his yokefellow in forming an inclined plane; only the *tail* of one and the *head* of the other formed the apex of the inclination, and gave an irresistibly comic feature to the turnout. Inside were the young people of the party, who, after getting shaken into their places, were found to consist of eight single ladies and as many young gentlemen, though the latter, if equal in numbers, were certainly in the minority in the confusion of tongues then reigning.

Following the ambulance came a close carriage more stylish in appearance than the other vehicles, but showing the same dissimilarity in the team, one side being drawn by a horse called by its master, who was something of a humorist, 'Thad Stevens,' and seeming as tall, gaunt, raw-boned and Roman-nosed as his namesake of Congressional memory is generally pictured by the Southern people; on the other by a sleek mule scarcely half as large as his partner. This contained two of the matrons of the party and a portion of the children, while a double buggy held the remainder. The rear was brought up by a baggage-wagon partly covered by a most dilapidated tent, and driven by a negro boy who could display more teeth, tongue and foot than any other member of the party.

Such, then, was the general appearance of the party that in the summer of '68 took its departure for Tallulah and Tocoa Falls, situated in Habersham County, in the North-east portion of Georgia, and whose adventures we intend to chronicle during a journey of more than a hundred miles.

The train had hardly reached the outskirts of the village on the high road to Athens, when an unexpected obstacle barred its further progress in that direction. The bridge over the Oconee river had been taken up for repairs and the stream was unfordable.. The result of a brief consultation was a deflection to the left for the Hog Mountain Road, a much longer route. But little did the merry party, whose sole aim was enjoyment, care for this, so they proceeded on their way, right merrily, keeping up a running fire of talk between the vehicles, and making the woods ring with song and laughter, the natural overflow of youthful hearts. Their road lay through the upper portion of Clark county, known in election returns as "Dark Corner Precinct," and fully deserving its name the travelers thought,—the country being covered with dense pine forests through which the narrow road wound its tortuous course—its dull monotony rarely broken by any object more interesting than a log cabin with its small patch of corn and collards. As the day grew warmer, the conversational powers of the company began to flag, or confine themselves to the occupants of their immediate vehicles. In the ambulance a motion was made that any one acquainted with any interesting incidents of the country through which they were passing should relate them for the entertainment of the crowd. All professed their ignorance except a tall young man with blue spectacles, who kept a discreet silence.

"I see Mr. Z—— has a tale to unfold," cried a merry girl who was sitting opposite to him, "so do give it to us without further begging."

"I have only a few scraps of history," he replied, "which may not prove interesting to the *novel* reading portion of the party, but still I will repeat them, for it is the duty of every Georgian to make himself familiar with the character and actions of those gallant spirits who stood by their county in the hour of her greatest extremity, and, in the contest for liberty, hazarded life and property. Most of you already know that this county in which you reside, was named after General Elijah Clark, one of the first of our revolutionary worthies; but few of you know anything of his history.

He was a North Carolinian by birth, but removed to Georgia and settled in Wilkes county in 1774. He made his first appearance in the *history* of Georgia as Captain of a wagon train which he bravely defended from a body of Indians. When the whole of this State and South Carolina were evacuted by the American forces, Clark alone kept the field, and made his name a terror to the British forces. He figured conspicously in most of the battles and skirmishes in those two States, rose rapidly in rank, and his merits as a soldier may be easily known by his being solicited by two European nations to join their service; but the love of freedom, and a persuasion that Heaven would favor the righteous course of the Americans, made him bear with patience the loss of property, the indignities offered the helpless females of his family, and reject all offers that would wean him from the cause he had espoused. In the battles of Jack's Creek, Walton county, 21st of Sept., 1787, he commanded the whites, numbering two hundred, while the Indians, amounting to eight hundred were led by Mc Gilvary, a half breed. The attack was made on the hill three miles east of the spot upon which Monroe now stands, by Clark, in three divisions. The battle commenced at 10 o'clock, and continued until sunset. The Indians were defeated, and the Americans buried their dead in a stream which has since been known as "Dead Man's Branch."

The speaker stopped here, but was urged to proceed by the same mischievous girl, who was suspiciously busy with pencil and paper, but declared she was only taking notes of Georgia history to enlighten the ignorant Virginians when she returned to her native State. Ignoring the irony contained in this speech, he continued: "I know nothing further in regard to Clark, but we are now on the borders of Jackson county, so called to perpetuate the memory of General James Jackson, an Englishman, who landed in Savannah in 1772, a penniless youth of fifteen. He entered the office of Samuel Farley as a law student, but soon laid aside his law-books and associated himself with a portion of the citizens who had resolved to break the chains of British slavery. In this organization, his enthusiasm, courage and talents soon led to distinction. The first time that he distinguished himself was in an attack upon Savannah by a fleet of vessels aided by land forces. A party of volunteers, among them Jackson, then only nineteen, proceeded to that portion of the river where the vessels lay aground, and set them on fire. After acting a conspicuous part in many of the battles in Geoegia, he retired at the close of the war with the rank of Colonel, married and settled in Savannah. He afterwards held almost every high office in Georgia, and became United States Senator. While in the last position he was one of the warmest opposers of the Yazoo Act, and it was chiefly through his influence that it was repealed. There is a tradition still existing among the Georgians, that, when the public officers were assembled at Louisville to burn the records of this dishonorable affair, a venerable man, whose head was white with the frost of fourscore years, suddenly appeared upon the square and commenced an address in which he said that he did not think that earthly fire should be employed to show the indignation of the people and taking a sun-glass from his bosom, he succeeded in igniting the papers with it, amidst a profound silence. He then retired as mysteriously as he appeared, and no traces of him could be afterwards found. Many believe this man to have been General Jackson, who had traveled from his distant home on horseback to witness the final destruction of a cause against which his feelings had been so warmly enlisted. He died in Washington City while serving as Congressman, and when he thought his death near he said that, if after death his heart was opened "Georgia" would be legibly read there. If a foreigner could feel such interest in the State of his adoption, how much greater the obligation for her sons to hold untarnished the fame of Georgia, and defend her, not only from foreign tyranny, but the still more insidious foes of political intrigue and corruption at home. In the words of the man of whom we have been speaking, "A free representation was what we fought for, a free representation was what we obtained; a free representation is what our children should be taught to lisp and our youths to relinquish only with their lives."

"Bravo," cried several voices, "I did not know you had such talents for stump oratory, old fellow," said a gentleman who sat by him, clapping the tall young man on the shoulder. "I should not wonder if we heard from you in the Legislature yet."

"I hope it will not be in a scallawag affair then," he replied laughing, and evidently rather pleased with the sensation he had produced.

"There is another position which I think Mr. Z—— would fill with even greater honor to himself, I beg to present him to the company in *propria persona*," said the young lady mentioned, a mischievous smile dimpling her face, as she handed around an envelope on which she had sketched a clever caricature of him as THE GEORGIA HISTORIAN.

The likeness was so striking as to bring a smile to every face, in which the sufferer good humoredly joined after a vain attempt to look dignified; though he vowed to be even with his tormentors at some future time.

"It is only a Roland for your Oliver," she said laughing merrily." "I saw your glance at *me* a while ago when you spoke of the *novel* reading portion of the company, and determined then to have my revenge."

"Ah! I see by your explanation that you are getting frightened at the wrath you have laid up for yourself," he said shaking his finger at her, "I dub you OUR SPECIAL ARTIST and shall keep this to illustrate my next history," and folding up the sketch he placed it in his pocket.

"Since both you and I have won a *soubriquet* this early in the trip. I insist that all the others shall take some name too, for it will wound my delicate sensibilities dreadfully if I should see in the book of travels, which you will publish on your return, myself merely mentioned as "our artist" while the rest are spoken of as the belle Miss T., the beauty Miss W., &c.

"I agree with you Madge, I have no desire to see my real name in print, so I will be called Meg Merrilles, so write me down Mr. Historian." "And I Die Vernon," said another. "Who will be Rashliegh Osbaldiston?" "I will," said one of the gentlemen, "must I promise—"To smile and be a villain still?" "Scott seems to be a favorite with you all, young ladies," said another, but I think I will patronize some other author. I will be Capitola Black, and will promise you to deliver you from all the Black Donalds you may encounter."

"I will be Miss Patty Pace, for I always thought I resembled her," said a little figure in the corner, "and now with all these pockets and my feather fan, the likeness is complete."

"I believe I will retain the nickname I gained the first time I ever visited Georgia," said a lady of uncertain age, but upon whose calm face the years of old maidenhood had not set their accustomed seal of peevishness and ill temper. "I will be Aunt Quimby still, and sometime, when we have nothing better to talk about, will tell you how I won the title."

"We have decided to be the Twin Sisters,—Manolia and Iolia," said two sentimental friends, "and W. and H. shall be Roscius and Julius. Perhaps we may be able to find the vale of Paradise where Manolia lived, for the scene of the book is laid at Tallulah."

"It had just as well have been laid anywhere else for the likeness it bears to the locality," said one of the matrons, who had visited the Falls before.

"Thank you for speaking Mrs. W., and thus reminding us to give the matrons names too---Lady Montague, Lady Capulet and Mrs. Page.

"You can easily find a Falstaff in our guide, but I am afraid your Romeo and Juliet for the first two to quarrel over will be missing, for there is not a pair of lovers in the party."

"The *morantic* scenes, as Widow Bedott would say, among which we are going may make some. Now for the gentlemen. The Historian, Roscius, Julius and Rashleigh Obaldistone, are already named, another shall be Falstaff, a 6th Lord Chesterfield, a seventh Don Quixote."

The children we will not name, as angels and cherubs are always nameless; and the seven wee specimens of humanity which we have with us all belong to those races of celestial beings, in their mother's eyes at least," said Aunt Quimby.

"I only hope they may retain their angelic character throughout the trip," said the Historian, "for they are generally the disturbing element in parties as well as families."

"There spoke the old bachelor," said Lady Montague, the good-natured mother of several of the children. "Some day you will call them well-springs of joy."

He shook his head incredulously, and just then Falstaff drove up, and, true to his character, asked if was not time to attend to the wants of the inner man, and proposed they should stop at a church they were approaching for their noontide rest, as there was a good spring near. This was readily agreed to, and the building soon came in sight, situated in a fine grove of trees. The horses were unharnessed and supplied with provender from the baggage wagon. The provision trunk, stocked with dainties of all kinds, was brought from the same receptacle; a white cloth spread beneath a shady tree, and the merry party gathered around to partake of the cold fare, for which no better condiments could have been found than the keen appetites, hearty laughter and merry jests which seasoned the informal meal.

"How are we to amuse ourselves for the next two hours," exclaimed Capitola, diving into the trunk for another cake. "The Ladies, Montague and Capulet, forbid all inroads upon the hams at this stage of our journey; and as I see the last of the seven chickens disappearing behind the down which Roscius would term a moustache, we will have to look out some more intellectual amusement than eating."

"I propose that we all get into the omnibus and persuade Aunt Quimby to give us a few sketches of a visit she made to Georgia when she was——"

"Young, you were going to say, Mary," said Aunt Quimby with a pleasant glance at the young girl's confused face. "You need not have been afraid to finish the sentence, I am not the least sensitive about my age; and as that old church up yonder strongly suggests some funny incidents that befell me at one very much like it, though situated in another county, I will readily comply with your request, if the others would like to hear them." There was a chorus of affirmative answers, and all the young people were soon seated in the ambulance, while the elders remained to give the negro drivers their dinners, dispose of the remains of the lunch, and, perhaps, take a sly dip into their snuff boxes.

CHAPTER II.

THE GEORGIA SERMON.

"Most of you have heard me speak of Meg Carlton, the much loved friend of my youth," said Aunt Quimby, plunging at once into her story. "We were raised on adjoining plantations for, Mr. Carlton once owned Tudor Hall, the old fashioned country homestead whose moss grown roof can be plainly seen from the window of my peculiar sanctum in my Virginia home, and from which I have often signalled to Meg with all the satisfaction, if not the dexterity, of the Signal Corps. A white handkerchief tied to the blind was the daily signal that the school children from our house had started to the rendezvous at the foot of the hill where we always met our companions from Tudor Hall; and proceeded in company to the old log school house situated about a mile down the valley, where all the children of the neighborhood, high and low, rich and poor, met to receive their daily qnantum of birch and books—frequently more of the first than the last—under the various pedagogues who from time to time bore the scepter of authority in that edifice of learning. Meg and I were near the same age and inseparable companions from our earliest youth. We were in the same classes, shared the rewards and punishments equally, and gained about the same amount of knowledge, which was not a very large quantity; for though entirely unlike in temper and disposition, we were fully agreed in our dislike of study, and expertness in eluding the vigilance of our teachers. Out of school we were the ringleaders of all the plays, we rode the same saplings, swung on the same grapevines, paddeled in the same "branch," skipped over the same hop-scot" rings and played "checques" on the same shawl—antiquated amusements at which the school girls of the present day, incipient belles in pinafores—would raise their hands in holy horror; but which to us, buoyant with health and spirits, were gayeties that never lost their zest.

Our childhood passed in this happy, careless fashion till Meg was nearly fourteen, and I only a year younger, then a succcession of unlooked for events changed the whole tenor of both our lives.

An old uncle of Mr. Carlton's, whom he had never seen since his boyhood, died and left him a plantation in Georgia, and, weary of the hard labor necessary to cultivate the rugged mountain region in which we lived, he determined to emigrate thither. About the same time, my two elder sisters who had hitherto, in their characters as the belles of the neighborhood, monopolized my mother's attention, married; one, a merchant in Baltimore, the other, a planter from the Eastern Shore; and, their fates being decided, she suddenly awoke to the fact that I was growing up a rough hoydenish country girl; and it was decided that I should be sent to my Aunt Venable in Richmond, to receive the polish of the best school in that city. As to *will* was to *do* with both Mr. Carlton and my mother, these resolutions were both carried into effect, and, ere many weeks, Meg and I were widely sundered, each surrounded by new scenes, and with no means of communication except the slow and tedious mail arrangements of those days. We managed however, to keep up with each others movements till the summer I was seventeen, when I left school to find Mr. Carlton a guest at our house, while he settled some business affairs which had brought him back. He bore positive commands from Meg that I should return with him to act as her bridesmaid in the Fall. This I was eager to do, and after some difficulty I succeeded in persuading my parents to allow me to go; Mr. Carlton promising to see me safely home again in the Spring. Traveling facilities were in a very imperfect state in those days, most of it being performed by stage coaches, so that it was the tenth day from the time we started when we reached the village where it had been arranged that Meg should meet us. She and her brother, a boy of twelve, had reached there the night before, and as we had breakfasted on the route, we were soon on our journey in the comfortable family carriage, and we had time to notice the favorable alterations time had made in our appearances, changing us both from hoydenish school girls, to dignified young ladies. But that the old affectionate familiarity was the same, was demonstrated by the glibness of our tongues as soon as the little reserve of meeting wore off.

"I am afraid you will think you are going into the backwoods sure enough, Queenie, when I tell you it is two days journey from Stone Mountain to our house," said Meg after sometime. "There are, besides, no hotel accommodations on the way, so Pa has arranged for us to stay all night with some acquaintances of his, whom I expect you will think the very oddest people you ever saw."

"If she is the girl I take her to be, she will respect their sterling worth of character in spite of their uncouth appearance and manners," said her father. "You will find education much less generally diffused, even among persons of property, in this State than in Virginia, Queenie; but I am sure you will like the warm hearted kindness of the people. There is far less of exclusiveness and pride in any circle than we are accustomed to there; and, in the section through which we will travel, the word "fashion" is an unknown sound."

From this the conversation branched off to other topics of mutual interest, and there was so much to hear and tell on each side that we had no idea of the distance we had traveled till Mr. Carlton drew out his watch and announced that we had made a drive of twenty miles, and we must be looking out for a suitable place to feed our horses, and partake of the lunch which his wife had provided for us.

About noon we reached a church almost the *fac simile*, of that one yonder, only a little more dilapidated at which Mr. Carlton decided it was best for us to stop as there was a fine spring near. There was evidently something going on inside the house for some of the windows were open, and groups of horses were tied around, variously equipped with male and female saddles.

"That is an odd tune, and a most endless hymn they are singing," I said to Meg, after listning some time to a low murmuring sound that issued from the building.

"They are preaching," she said laughing, while Mr. Carlton added—

"That is another of the wonders of Georgia with which you will have, to become acquainted." "It is the *whang doodle* style of delivery. If you and Meg feel like it, we will go in and listen while the horses are resting."

This I was eager to do, so after finishing our lunch we entered.

The house was a small wooden edifice, the rough beams inside forming excellent resting places for the wasps, which buzzed about in a lively manner. It was about half filled with persons; the feminine element in pink and yellow calico, sunbonnets, and homespun dresses, largely predominating over the masculine, in suits of butter-nut yellow. The entrance door, like most of the country churches in Georgia, was placed by the side of the pulpit, so that we were obliged to enter facing the congregation, and our appearance created quite a sensation, judging from the nudging of elbows among the females, and the battery of eyes leveled upon us.

We had scarcely taken seats, when the preacher, a large stout man, dressed in homespun, suddenly paused in his harangue, and took his seat. His place was immediately filled by a thin wiry looking little man, with a set of very ugly features, which he contrived to make still more homely by continued grimaces and contortions. A whispered conference now took place between him and an old man in a white cloth skull cap who was as I afterwards learned, one of the deacons of the church. The old man seemed to be urging something to which the preacher appeared to object, and another brother was signalled for and approached. The three laid their heads together for some time, then the preacher turned away, and uttered such a deep and prolonged groan that I, at first, thought he was in bodily pain, but soon concluded it was only his manner of expressing his sense of the solemnity of the occasion. He took a deep draught of water from the bucket in front of the pulpit, after which he turned and addressed to the congregation—

"Brethering and sistering, I had not thought of trying to preach to you to-day, especially as I am powerful puny, but, as Brother Jenkins thinks it best, I will try to do as well as my weak back will allow. The brethren will please sing a hymn, as I would like to look over my text, as such highfalutin people have come to hear me preach."

We were a good deal amused to hear ourselves styled *highfalutin*, and were afraid to glance at Mr. Carlton, who had found a seat in the amen corner, and sat bolt upright looking as grave as a priest.

A brother near the pulpit now arose and mentioned the number of a hymn, which he requested might be "pitched purty high, and sung purty pert." Another brother raised it to a tune consisting of a succession of falls and quavers, which, Meg afterwards told me, was called the "Georgia Quibble."—The females joined in, every one singing 'high, tribble,' as they denominate the part now known as *tenor*. One woman just in front of us, who held a baby about six months old dressed in a black calico dress with a quilling of wide white lace around the low neck and short sleeves, was so energetic in the chorus that her comb fell out, and a shock of red hair came tumbling down on her shoulders. No wise disconcerted, however, by these *contretemps*, she turned around, and, without a word, popped the baby down in Meg's lap, who did not have time to reject the burden if so disposed, and running her hand in her pocket, produced a horn comb with which she proceeded to arrange her hair with as much coolness and deliberation as if in the privacy of her own chamber; meanwhile, not relaxing her addition to the volume of sound, which threatened to split our ear-drums.

The chorus they repeated so often that Meg and I learned it, and amused ourselves by singing it during the evening, and trying to imitate the peculiar manner in which the last word was drawn out.

We'll all rise together in that morning,
In that m-o-r-n-i-n-g—
In that m-o-r-n-i-n-g,
We'll all rise together in that morning.

When this was at last finished, the woman before us deigned to relieve Meg of the baby, who had remained perfectly quiet, staring with wide open eyes at the strange face above it, where confusion struggled with a desire to laugh, and it was well for me, that I could serene my face with the folds of my travelling vail, for, accustomed to the strict observances of the Episcopal church, the whole affair struck me in a far more ridiculous light than it did Meg.

The preacher now arose, only his head and shoulders being visible above the high pepper-box shaped pulpit, while the former was in dangerous proximity to a large beam that traversed the house from end to end, but he had, probably grown expert in the art of dodging, as he never once struck it, though gesticulating violently at times. He commenced in a sing-song tone interrupted by frequent blowings of the nose—

"My dear brethren and sisteren and lovely congregation, the words of my text is "In Heaven thar are many Mansions," which means houses, you know, and you will find it somewhar in the lids of this book. My lovely congregation, it makes me feel mighty bad when I see you all squeezing and scroughing in this little house; but, Oh! brethern, I have one conserlation, and it is a good one, for you know the good song we have just sung; but I must tell you what consoles me while I see you all scrouged in this little house made by earthly hands—I tell you, brethern, when we all get to Heaven, there will be no scroughing thar—Oh! sisteren, Heaven is a big place—it will hold all of us—it is as big as all around here by Shadmore, round by Brother Higginbottom's, cross through Dunkington, and away round thar. It must be that big, or it would never hold all the houses that the text talk about being in it—for it says, "In Heaven thar are many houses."—Then when we get thar we'll have the company of Jesus.—You have all hern a powerful sight about this man Christ Jesus, but I think I know a leetle more about him than any of you. He is not a great big man, like Brother Lambert, over thar, but a little slim, tall, spry looking fellow, like Brother Thacker over here, for my darter Jerusha says so, and she's book larned—

"Let's go, Meg," I whispered, "or I shall disgrace myself by laughing out in meeting." She nodded, and we made our way out; my unsettled gravity being by no means restored by a remark of young man, standing outside of the door, in regard to Meg's black silk dress—"My gosh, Jim, how do you suppose she stands all that stuff? Why the button-holes of my Sunday vest are worked with silk, and it almost swulters me to death."

Once at a safe distance from the house, we gave full vent to the laughter which had been gathering for the past hour, and we had not composed our features when Mr. Carlton joined us with a mischievous twinkle in his eyes. "Well, Queenie, what do you think of our Georgia preaching?" was his first query.

"I think it positive sacrilege to listen to such," I responded with all the heat of seventeen years.

"There you are mistaken, my dear," he said kindly. „In the essentials that go to make up the Christian character, patience, meekness, charity, love to one another, you will hardly find more shining examples in the largest and most intellectual church in Richmond than in the one we have just left. I know the preacher personally—He is, I believe, a sincere christian; and he ought to be the best man in the world, for he knows nothing but what the Lord has taught him."

"You think that is precious little, do you not, Queenie?" said Meg with another laugh in which Mr. Carlton joined.

"We will at least try to remember what the Bible says—that God has chosen the weak things of this world to confound the wise," said her father as we drove off, the last sound that reached our ears being the sing-song voice of the preacher repeating, "My dear brethren and sisteren, and lovely congregation."

"You will think you have come to a good country in which to laugh and grow fat, Queenie," he added when we were out of sight of the church, "You and Meg will have to lay in store a new stock of gravity for this evening, or you will never get through the night creditably."

And when night came, and we reached our stopping place, I realized the truth of his words. "But of the adventures that befell me there, I must tell you some other time," said Aunt Quimby, "for they are harnessing the horses for another start and we must gather up our things."

CHAPTER III.

"I think Aunt Quimby is disposed to be rather severe on the peculiarities of us "Georgians" said Don Quixote when they were once more settled in the ambulance and the procession in motion. "I shall take up a lance in our defence."

"It will be second tilting at windmills then, for no one can have a more thorouh respect and admiration for the Georgians than I have," she replied quickly. "The sermon I have repeated is very little more ridiculous than some I have heard in Virginia in years gone by. There was a Primitive Baptist, or as the Georgians would say, a "Hardshell," preacher in our neighborhood when I was a child, whose sermons furnished an inexhaustible fund of amusement to all who heard them. He and his wife were widely known by their nicknames of "Watty" and "Pricy," taken from their manner of abbreviating each others names, Walter and Priscilla, and I suppose two greater oddities never sustained to each other the relation of man and wife. Their attendance on an Association in Baltimore when they were old people, on which occasion Watty wore a full suit of yellow nankeen ornamented with immense brass buttons, and Pricy appeared in a bright pink silk dress and two bonnets on her head at the same time, is still laughed over by those who witnessed it.

Once when Watty was very sick, the doctor recommended smothered chicken as a good diet, and on his next visit inquired of Pricy if his patient had relished it.

"Sakes alive! he haint took it yit," she replied, "I put the rooster between two big feather-beds soon this mornin', but the pesky thing wont git smothered no way."

I have often heard my father laugh about Watty having invited him home with him from church one Sunday, saying that he had told Pricy about the nice stuffed chicken he had eaten at our house a short time before, and she had promised to have some just like it for dinner that day. To gratify the old man, Pa went, and when they took their seats at the table, there, indeed, was the stuffed chicken, but with an odd look about it, which Pricy explained by apologizing for stuffing it with *blue* wool, as she had no *white*.

"Such anecdotes of these old people are almost numberless," she added, when the laugh had subsided, "but these are enough to prove that oddities are not confined to Georgia, and without regard to place, I "shoot folly as she flies."

"Then give Mrs. Gummidge a bullet and wake her up," whispered Cap, "for her face looks like young birds' heads—all eyes."

"Young puppies, rather," said Roscius in the same tone, but the whisper reached the ears of the good lady, the scape-goat of this otherwise "ower true tale" brought her to a perpendicular immediately, and gave her occasion to remark that she was more than ever convinced that she was "a lone, lorn cretur, with everybody agin her."

The badinage which this provoked lasted for several miles, for when people are pleased with themselves and each other, it does not take much wit to create amusement. Then their arriva at a long, and rather rickety bridge, which the elders thought had better be crossed on foot, created a diversion; and when the carriages were refilled, it was found that there had been a general changing of places. The Historian had taken charge of the double buggy, containing Lady Montague and four of the children, thus creating a partial vacuum in the ambulance, which its remaining occupants took advantage of, to dispose themselves in various easy positions to enjoy the *siesta*, that the sultry afternoon made desirable. Falstaff, having taken Miss Quimby in his buggy, once more led the van, making for Jefferson, the county seat of Jackson county. So rapidly did he advance, that all the vehicles were left behind except the carriage, which managed to keep in sight.

Meanwhile, the shades of evening were beginning to creep on, and the clouds which had altogether obscured the sun, began to descend in slow-falling drops, that soon obliged Miss Quimby to vacate her seat in the buggy for one in the carriage; and still the anxious looks cast back from every eminence, failed to reveal any signs of the missing vehicles.—Falstaff, at length, paused for consultation with the occupants of the carriage. He expressed a fear lest the other vehicles had taken a wrong road, and, as it would be impossible for them to reach Jefferson at the slow rate they were then traveling, he proposed that they should stop at the first convenient house, and endeavor to obtain accommodations for the night, which promised to be so rainy as to preclude all chance of using the tents, for the ladies and children at least.

The matrons readily agreed to his proposition; and then commenced an anxious lookout for the desired haven, but no suitable place presented itself for several miles.

At length they reached a moderate sized house with a large grove in front of the gate, and after some chaffering with the owner, he agreed to let the party have the use of one room, and the piazza. They were all so weary that even these poor accommodations were welcome. The horses were unharnessed, and Lady Capulet and Mrs. Page busied themselves inspecting their quarters and transferring the loose articles from the carriage to the house; still keeping an anxious lookout for their companions, and, especially, for the baggage-wagon, which contained the supplies for both man and beast. Just as Falstaff was about starting back in search of them, they hove in sight. The Historian was driving in solitary state in the double buggy, the breakage of a shaft having necessitated the transfer of its load to the ambulance, and a very slow rate of traveling.

Amidst a good deal of confusion occasioned by the rain, which began now to pour in torrents, the eatables, bed-clothes and other baggage were transferred to the house, and the party made preparations to make themselves as comfortable as circumstances would permit. But now the first damper was cast over their spirits by the indisposition of one of the children, and the tears and lamentations of its mother, who, forgetting everything else in maternal solicitude, declared that she was determined to return home in the morning.

Every one wore long faces, at this prospective disarrangement of their plans, but Mrs. Gummidge, true to her character of rising superior to difficulties, declared that they all only needed a cup of hot coffee to revive their spirits, and diving into the provision trunk for the materials, started on an exploring expedition for the means of making it. These were found in the kitchen, situated nearly fifty yards from the house, and only to be reached by means of two very large slabs raised one or two feet from the ground. It was no easy matter to walk these in the pitchy darkness which then preveiled, and Roscius and Die Vernon, who had volunteered their assistance to Mrs. Gummidge, found themselves by a miss-step pitched head-foremost into the muddy yard beneath; but after some scrambling, and much laughter, a large pot of coffee was made and dispensed by means of tin-cups; other eatables, already cooked, were produced from the trunk, and a hearty meal restored the spirits of the party to their natural level. The matrons went off to bed, and the young people gathered on the piazza to amuse themselves.

A better selected party for such a trip could rarely have been met with. The masculine portion, ranging in age from forty-five to fifteen, were all gentlemen in the strictest sense of the term; free from dissipation of all kinds, and uniting a sufficient degree of good looks and intelligence with much of the frankness and bonhomie of manner peculiar to the Southern character; while the young ladies, though all gay and good looking, possessed sufficient diversity of age, appearance and disposition to make their companionship agreeable to all the gentlemen, as well as each other. The matrons were "wisest, discreetist, best," and just old enough for their experience to prove a balance power to the impetuosity of the younger portion without marring their enjoyment of a single pleasure; and both young and old met on the common ground of familiar acquaintanceship, and thorough good will. Such being the case, the hours sped by rapidly in jest and song and it was late before a proposition was made to retire.

"Let me beg you to remain a few minutes, ladies," said the Historian, "to decide a grave question which has been weighing upon my mind all the evening."

Then when all stood around him expectantly, he gravely requested them to decide among themselves which should have the honor of shaving off his beard in the morning.

"Truly, that is "giving to airy nothing a local habitation and a name," exclaimed Meg Merrilles, while Capitola suggested that it was probalble a cat could be found on the premises that would relieve them of the trouble. The others followed up the attack so successfully that he soon began to cry quits, and beat a retreat by going to the carriage to look for a missing blanket.

The gentlemen disposed themselves to sleep in the piazza and hall, and the ladies and children, fourteen in number, packed themselves away in double rows upon the floor of a room scarcely twelve by fourteen feet; the single bed which it contained being given up to the sick child and two of the matrons.

The elders and children were already asleep, but were roused by the meriment of the girls in making down their bed, which consisted of single blankets spread on the bare floor, and a row of carriage cushions for their heads. After much chattering and discussion, they were all placed for the night, except Miss Patty Pace, who, in moving around, contrived to upset a pan of water which flowing under the sleepers, produced a general scrambling and confusion.

The water being disposed of by sweeping into the fire-place, and Miss Patty Pace having retired into silence and her wet blanket, quiet reigned for an hour or two, only broken by an occasional groan from some sleeper at her failure to find the soft side of her plank. About twelve, however, a quevelous voice was heard complaining that one of the children in the upper row had taken off her water-fall with its toe.

The search for the missing article roused up all the sleepers, and there was a chorus of complaints of cold and discomfort, and a scramble for the few bed-cloths, amid which the motion was given to turn by right flank, which was performed in a creditable manner. The matrons then commanded silence, and threatened to give whoever spoke what Paddy gave the drum; but whispered jokes and smothered laughter proved that the gayety of the younger portion was unsubdued; and when one of the elders in her efforts to suppress the noise began to belabor Meg Merrilles, who was asleep, and, therefore innocent, the fun burst all bounds and exploded in an irrepressible shout of laughter, which roused even the gentlemen from their uneasy slumbers in the piazza. They found that the rain had ceased, and, as day was beginning to break, preparations were made for departure; it having been determined to take advantage of the cool of the morning to travel, and not breakfast till they reached Jefferson.

The ladies made hasty toilets before the single looking-glass belonging to the party, and came out looking as fresh as if they had a good night's rest. An hour's travel brought them to Jefferson, a neat village prettily situated on a hill bordering the Oconee river, and containing a court house, jail, two hotels, one church, one academy, and five stores.

As it was the plan of the party to combine economy with pleasure, they did not stop at either of the hotels, but having obtained permission to cook their breakfasts in a kitchen on the outskirts of the town, the ladies with their wonderful adaptibility to circumstances, pinned up their dresses, and set to work in earnest.

The owner of the house, a hard-working woman who kept no servant, took a fancy to the party as soon as she discovered they were not gay lillies who could neither toil nor spin, and rendered them such efficient aid that by the time the carriage was mended a bountiful meal of hot biscuits, coffee and fried ham smoked upon the table, which the hostess had insisted upon covering with a cloth; and though the table furniture was various, a tin bucket serving for a butter plate, a bag for a sugar bowl, it was doubtful whether any meal, although served by Soyer, was ever eaten with greater gusto.

By eight o'clock the dishes had been washed and repacked, their hostess thanked, and more substantially rewarded for her trouble, and they were *en route* for Gainsville, distant twenty miles. The roads were heavy from the recent rains, and the party jogged along in rather a soberer mood than usual. Some even took sly naps in convenient corners of the carriages, quite unmindful of the contortions of face and form which were the consequence of their uneasy positions, till a sudden jolt of the ambulance sent Capitola so far from the perpendicular that her waterfall came unfastened, and, rolling down in her lap, disclosed three rats, so like the natural ones, that the Historian drew his knife to defend himself from the hairy monsters.

"Is that the waterfall that there was such a hue and cry raised about last night?" asked Lord Chesterfield, so far forgetting the dignity belonging to his name, as to laugh heartily.

"Yes; some one divested me of it while I was asleep," said Cap, coolly proceeding to stow the rats away in her pocket, and with a toss of her head skaking her own hair in natural ringlets upon her shoulders. "The reason it came off just now was because I did not have two glasses to see the back part of my head this morning."

"That is to see yourself as ithers see you," said Don Quixote. "It is a strange thing to me that ladies will take so much trouble and wear so many outlandish and uncomfortable things on their heads, when I never saw a gentleman yet who did not admire a simple dress and coiffure more than the most elaborate style."

"My dear sir," exclaimed Die Vernon, "you surely do not delude yourself with the thought that we take the trouble you speak of to please the tastes of *your* sex? I assure you, if there were none but masculine critics of our appearance, our toilet tasks would be very easy; but it is our dear feminine friends with their keen eyes, wonderful memories, and sharp tongues, whose criticisms we dread."

"Because you know they are up to all the tricks of the trade, and cannot be half so easily humbugged as we poor masculines," said Lord Chesterfield. "I do not think, however, that Don ought to complain of the attention you pay to the toilet,—I am in favor of allowing you even more time for these mysterious rites; for I agree with a friend of mine who made a speech at Emory College this year. He said he was a woman's right's man, and there was one privilege of which she had been deprived for years, that he never intended to miss an opportunity of insisting that she should have, though it had not yet appeared in the list of grievances set forth by any strong-minded female. It was *his* candid opinion, in which *I* concur, that a woman has just as much right as a man—to comb her head everyday."

"Since even *Lord Chesterfield* grows witty at our expense," said Meg Merrilles, "I propose that we surrender to him another of our rights—that of having the last word—acknowledge ourselves vanquished, and retire to bury our dead. Do, Aunt Quimby, give us another of your funny stories to make us forget our defeat."

"From the looks of a memorandum book which I saw Miss Quimby writing in this morning, I am sure she could furnish us with a variety of tales, both new and old," said the Historian, "and I propose that we elect her our Scheherezade, and insist that she give us a story every *day*, or *night*, as she may prefer."

"I am glad that my task will only extend over *ten*, instead of a *thousand* nights," said Aunt Quimby, "and I will agree to what you propose, on condition that when we reach the mountains, and have something better to occupy our minds, I may rest from my labors."

"Agreed," cried several voices. "Now consider yourself the story teller of the Mutual Admiration society, and proceed to give us so more of your "Georgia Scenes."

"I find the outlines of the stories you wish written out in my memorandum book, and I will read them aloud, only adding from memory what may be omitted here," she remarked opening her book. "In order to a full understanding of them, I will have to begin where I left off yesterday. I think we had just left the church where I had heard my first Georgia Sermon.

CHAPTER IV.

THE GEORGIA HOMESTEAD.

We traveled rapidly on for several hours over a country which bore little resemblance to my ideal Southland. In all my dreams, and they had been many since I had decided to visit Georgia, I had pictured it a land of fragrance and bloom, where every breeze wafted the breath of the orange and myrtle groves, and perpetual summer reigned; nor had the tantalizing glimpses of scenery, caught through the windows of the fast revolving car, entirely put to flight these ideal fancies.—The pine barrens of North Carolina with their seried ranks of trees, pierced with innumerable death wounds; the fertile rice fields of South Carolina, interspersed with cypress swamps, draped in their mantles of grey moss; the cotton fields of Southern Georgia, hoary as the head of age, had been alike novel and interesting to me. *Now*, even these elements of the picturesque were wanting. The road wound through a barren and uncultivated country, acres of worn out commons alternating with rugged hills, covered with a dense growth of pines, interspersed with oak, gum, and hickory, the hardy forest trees to which I was accustomed in my mountain home, their richly variegated leaves showing that, even in October, the frost had begun to use his magic pencil in Georgia; while as the sun declined, the air grew so chilly as to render comfortable the heavy traveling shawl which my mother had insisted upon my bringing with me. There were no signs of human habitation, except an occasional log cabin, and I was beginning to wonder silently as to the distance to our stopping place for the night when Meg, who had noticed my weariness, announced that we were very near it; and in a few moments an abrupt turn in ihe road brought us directly in front of a building placed with its back almost against the high hill we had just descended, and one end so near another of equal size that there seemed no outlet from the hollow in which it stood, save by the road over which we had come.

The foundations of the house comsisted of slabs supported at the corners by large blocks of wood, and on each end of these rooms, closely resembling pens, were formed by notched logs; while the space in the middle, answering the purpose of a passage, was open at each end, and enabled the beholder to look directly through into the garden behind the house, where the only vegetation was a growth that I took to be young palmetto trees, but which I afterwards found to be "blue collards," plants indigenous to Georgia, and therefore strangers to me. A low, sloping roof covered this unique dwelling, and from the rough rock chimney at each end, a thin stream of blue smoke clurled up above the forest trees that filled the yard.

The stopping of the carriage was the signal for the appearance of about half a score of tow-headed children, who peeped at us shyly around the corners and from the windows, and about the same number of small dogs of various shades of yellow, that barked and snapped around with such a clamor, as to vividly recall the memory of Scott's Pepper and Mustard breed and left little hope of a peaceful descent from the carriage.

The yelping crew were, however, quickly put to flight by the appearance of a stout grey-haired man, not unlike Dandie Dinmont, save that the "hodden gray" was replaced by a full suit of "butternut," as the yellowish brown procured from the bark of the hickory is termed in Georgia. He approached the carriage, and greeting Mr. Carlton familiarly by the title a brother, while he looked curiously at Meg and me.

"You see I have brought my girls according to promise, Judge," said Mr. Carlton, presenting him to us by the name of Thigpen.

"The women folks will be powerful tickled to see them," he

responded, giving each of us a grip that made my fingers tingle. "Light and walk in."

"If this is one of the Judges, what must the common people be?" I thought as I descended, visions of the learned and famous men who held that position in Virginia, passing through my mind. I did not know then, that every second man in this State bears some such title, though of no higher rank than Magistrates at home.

"I hope they will give us roast turkey for supper," whispered Meg as we made our way over the fence that surrounded the yard, calling my attention to a large flock that were disposing themselves for the night among the branches of one of the trees, which was the most homelike feature of the scene.

"At the door we were met by a small, thin-faced woman dressed in blue and yellow homespun—who declared in shrill tones that she was powerful glad to see us, and led the way into a long, low room, which, though containing a bed, was evidently the best room in the house. One end was occupied by an immense fire-place filled with blazing hickory logs, and the persons sitting around it were formally presented to us as Miss Civilia Margarita Bernice Thigpen, Miss Eurydine Alvira Thigpen, and Miss Atalanta Samantha Thigpen, each high sounding name being uttered in Mrs. Thigpen's shrillest tones, and followed by a series of bobs, or old fashioned courtesies, from each of the owners.

Meg and I were both glad to hide our amusement under the excuse of laying aside our wrappings. These disposed of, we were installed in the warmest seats by the fire, and were at liberty to look at the ladies to whom we had been introduced. The two that sat next us, were evidently twins, and rather pretty girls in spite of their sallow complexions, the result, as I afterwards learned, of their excessive use of strong coffee and snuff. They were dressed in blue homespun, and their hair was parted in the middle behind, coiled in a tight roll back of each ear, and held in place by burnt straws.—Though looking to be about seventeen, they were evidently considered children by their elder sister, whose appearance was so remarkable as to deserve a paragraph to herself.

Miss Civilia Margarita Bernice Thigpen was a tall angular woman of an uncertain age, with high cheek bones, lantern-jaws, and a shock of rusty black hair which was combed up to the very crown of her head and tied with a shoe string, the brass tips of which dangled down behind. It was then wound round loosely, very nearly like it is worn at the present day, the centre of the coil being occupied by a large bunch of chrisanthemums, and other gay colored autumn flowers. The dress which accompanied this remarkable head gear, was a bright, red calico with sprawling yellow flowers running over it, and was made with a very slack back, and very full forebody, ending in an extremely long point, around which the narrow, red ribbon that encircled her waist was carefully pinned, and fell in long ends to the top of the deep flounce trimmed with home-made cotton edging that ornamented the bottom of the skirt. This unique costume was completed by an embroidered collar of the largest size, trimmed with wide cotton lace, enormous pinchbeck earrings, and half-handed blue cotton mits.

"You need not look so incredulous, Die, I am not drawing on my fancy, but describing a veritable dress," said Aunt Quimby, pausing to look around. "And the wearer is still living, I expect, for she seemed to be in a whit-leather state."

"Long may she wave," said the Historian. "But proceed, for I am interested in her."

"The original of the portrait I have drawn sat bolt upright in her chair knitting, as if for life, on a blue woolen sock, and only answering in monosyllables the remarks in regard to the weather and similar topics which Meg and I forced ourselves to make, after the first stunning effect of her appearance had passed off. At length, when Meg in her efforts to make conversation, inquired as to the amusements of the neighborhood, she burst forth in shrill nasal tones as if obliged to speak.

"Why, in the summertime we have camp-meetings, and in the winter lasses-lickins and quiltings. I was at one last night in this beat, and we had lots of taffy and goobers, and a powerful sight of fun."

Having said her say she relapsed into silence, knitting faster than before, and Meg and I retired behind our pocket handkerchiefs, afraid to trust our voices to make a single comment; and it was a relief when Mr. Carlton and his host entered.— Then another succession of bobs took place, after which the twins disappeared in the direction of the kitchen. Mr. Carlton and Mr. Thigpen struck up an animated discussion on the culture of cotton, the one inexhaustible topic of Southern conversation; and, having nothing better to do, I allowed my eyes to wander round the room, noting each article of furniture. The bed whose feather glories rose to a climax in the middle, and were covered with a quilt whose stars of red and yellow calico were supposed to represent the splendors of the rising sun; the tall pile of similar efforts of genius packed on a chair in one corner; the white curtains with their cotton ball fringe; the rag carpet that covered the floor, all spoke of cleanliness and thrift; and I found myself wondering if simplicity naturally tended to barrenness of mind, and, with the glowing fancy of eighteen summers, I was beginning to paint a life like this with one kindred soul, when a door opened behind me and Meg whispered—"Behold the coming man," and I turned to add one more to the list of originals which this family had furnished.

Had Dickens ever visited Georgia, I should believe that he had found in the being, formally presented to us as Mr. Isaac Adolphus Thigpen, and familiarly termed "Ikey" by his family, the original of "Sloppy" in Our Mutual Friend. There was certainly "too much of him longwise, too little of him broadwise, and too many angles of him anglewise." His long head, covered with thin, tow colored hair, was set so far forward on his neck that his protruding jaw seemed resting on his bosom, and he looked up at you through his scant eyebrows, which certainly offered but few obstructions to his sight. His arms were unusally long, and, as George Carlton afterwards said, he would have been thundering tall if he had not crooked so far at the bottom; and it was no wonder that he suffered so much with cold, when there was so much of him on the ground, in the shape of splay feet. These ungainly members were now clad in cowhide boots that had never known blacking, and he had evidently donned for our special benefit, the red silk neck tie which made the faded hues of his butternut suit more dingy by contrast.

This uncouth figure made for a chair near us by a series of spasmodic jerks, which reminded me of the antics of a "supple sawnee," and, having sidled into it, and stared, first Meg and then me, out of countenance, he opened his lips and spake:

"They tell me you come all the way from Virginny?" with a sidelong glance at me. "I reckon you seen some sights of towns on your way."

I assented, mentioning Richmond and Augusta as being the largest cities on the route.

"Well, Comin and Gainesville is the onliest towns I ever seen, but I've got a brother that's livin in Atlanty" he answered, as if this last fact was sure to raise him in our estimation.

"I tell you he is a smart boy too," broke in Miss Civilia "He can read Greek and Laturn jest about as easy as I can Comly's Reader, and it would do you a powerful sight a good to hear how beautiful he can speak; it farly brings tears to my eyes; and as for goodness, he's been pious from his very *cradlehood*, I do believe."

"I am afraid he will lose it all in Atlanty, it is such a big, wicked place," said her mother, who had come in. "I never wanted him to go, and when he," nodding her head at her husband, I would send him, I *bellowed*, and I tell you, I *bellowed powerful too*."

The announcement of supper by one of the children here put a stop to the good lady's flow of talk, and gave us an opportunity of indulging in a quiet laugh while passing out to it. The meal was laid in the same room in which it had been cooked, in an out building in the yard. If tables ever *groan* the one before us, was fairly entitled to *shriek* from the weight of things laid upon it, though it did not contain Meg's anticipated roast turkey. In its place was a baked possum, its head twisted round so that it lay in its natural position with its sharp face and grinning teeth staring at you over its back. It was flanked on one side by a large dish of cold vegetables, beans, cabbage and potatoes, and on the other by an immense chicken pie, wonderfully ornamented around the edges by impressions of fingers and thumbs. Between these dishes and the set of delf ware at the head, not an inch of the table cloth was allowed to be visible, the spaces between the principal plates of biscuits, loaf-bread, hocakes and gingerbread being filled by saucers of preserves, pickles, custards, pies and cheese. In the middle of the table was a large bowl containing butter enough to supply a medium sized family for a week, but upon my requesting to be helped to some, Mrs. Thigpen exclaimed: "Oh, don't take any butter yet; that's to eat with the hot sweet tater biscuits, and flipper jacks,—they'll be along presently."

I subsided quickly, well aware that the pulmonary symptoms that at once afflicted Meg, Mr. Carlton and George, would prove contagious if I attempted to speak.

This array of edibles, lavish at it was, failed to provoke very keen appetites among our party, and we did not linger very long over the table, in spite of the hospitible entreaties of the family for us "to make out our suppers." Once more settled in the best room, Miss Civilia, after offering us a dip from her snuff box, produced a cheap accordeon from a closet, and learning that neither Meg nor I performed on that instrument, seated herself and began to play the air of "'Tis said that Absence Conquers Love," accompanying the instrument with her voice, and rolling up her eyes till nothing but the whites were visible. It was hard to tell which was the most shrill and discordant, the accordeon or her voice, and it was a relief to our auditory nerves, as well as risibles, when Mrs. Thigpen's sharp tones interposed at the conclusion of the piece.

"Well, Civilia Margarita Bernice, you can play some more

arter awhile, now I want to talk awhile with the gals, while you and the twinses do up the jobs."

Miss Civilia looked half inclined to rebel, but finally shut up the accordeon, and stalked out of the room evidently in high displeasure.

"She's a powerful techy cretur," said her mother looking after her, "and we all have to be mighty careful how we talk to her, I think its from her having the pleumony so bad in her head. I tell you she's dredful bad off sometimes. But lor sakes! she's powerful smart for all that, and does lots of work. I must just show you some of her quilts,"—and going to the pile in the corner she commenced taking them down, and spreading them on the bed for our inspection, discoursing all the time on the beauties and merits of Irish-chain, rising-sun, nine-diamond, log-cabin, and sunflower patterns, with a volubity and originality that kept us all constantly amused.

This display lasted until the hands of the clock pointed to eight, when Mr. Carlton proposed that we should retire, as he wished to make an early start in the morning. To this we readily agreed, and were shown into a small back room containing two beds, and one or two long blue chests. In one of the former Meg and I were soon ensconced, and free to give vent to the laughter which had been gathering all the evening; but we were too weary to indulge much, even in this, and were just dropping to sleep when the door opened to admit a strange procession. First, came Miss Civilia, bearing aloft a very consumptive looking tallow candle, and followed by Mrs. Thigpen and the "two twinses" all bearing under their arms what, at first sight, seemed to me bags of cotton, but which turned out to be children of various sizes in different stages of somnolence. They deposited their burdens at the other end of the room, and, going out, returned several times similarly laden, till curiosity induced me to raise up to see how they were disposing of them.

"Oh! Meg," I whispered horror struck," they are putting the children in the chests."

"Well, I thought they would have to pack them away in some such place unless this was a gutta percha house," she responded, sleepily. "If they shut down the lids there will a second 'Murder of the Innocents."'

The whole affair struck me as so ludicrous, that it was several hours before I could again compose myself to sleep; and it seemed as if we had just closed our eyes when we were aroused by Miss Civilia's sharp tones informing us that breakfast was ready, though very few signs of day had yet penetrated our room. A hasty toilet and breakfast followed, and, at sum: so we bade farewell to the Thigpens I, at least, never expecting to see them again; but I reckoned without my host, as the sequel will show. Now I see that Falstaff is stopping for dinner, so we will postpone the remainder till some more convenient season.

CHAPTER V.

Falstaff had the carriage drawn up under the shade of some large trees by the side of the road preparatory to taking dinner; but scarcely had the company alighted, when the rain began to fall heavily, and there was a general scramble for places in the ambulance. This vehicle proving insufficient, however, for the accommodation of the party, two of the gentlemen were sent to a house on the oposite side of the road to ask shelter for the ladies and children. After a considerable time they returned to report that no living thing was to be seen on the place, except a few fowls and hogs. This was the more remarkable, as it was a fine building situated immediately on the side of the road, only a small yard separating it from the public highway, and the open doors and windows showed no attempt at security.

The ladies, moved, the gentlemen declared, more by the failing that proved fatal to mother Eve, than any desire of protection from the rain, formed themselves into an investigating committee to explore this enchanted castle, whose inmates seemed bound by some invisible spell; and putting the matrons at the head, marched over in solid phalanx. The front door stood wide open, showing a long hall with several closed doors on either side, which yielded readily to the touch, and they peeped into the rooms over each others shoulders, evidently expecting to find each one a Blue Beard's chamber; but nothing met their eyes except plain articles of furniture in rather greater disorder than is usual in the apartments of tidy housekeepers. The upper rooms were entirely bare, both of furniture and inmates, and they returned to the piazza to find the gentlemen comfortably settled in the chairs which it contained, and ready to laugh at them for their ill success.

"Confess, young ladies, that you expected to find a handsome young Prince secreted in some of the rooms of this mysterious house, who would immediately fall captive to the charms of some one of you!" said the Historian. "Under what head shall I place this incident in my book of travels?"

"As a *Dear Hunt*, of course," said Capitola. "That is what people said we were going to the mountains for."

"I am afraid the *dear* caught here will not prove a royal buck," said Meg, "from the look of some clothes hanging in one of the rooms. They were certainly not purple and fine linen. I think I shall wait till I get to the Falls to do my hunting, perhaps, I may catch the Hermit in my toils."

"Well, I propose we 'use the gifts the gods provide," said the Historian, "and take our dinners on this piazza. Perhaps when its savory odors reach the Lares and Penates of this household, they may speak and solve the mystery that surrounds it."

This proposition was acceded to by the others, as the rain still continued; the provision trunk was brought, and they made a merry meal; the Historian proving the life of the party, and keeping them constantly amused by his oddities. He declared that he believed the owner of the place must be a fairy princess, and he thought he would remain and see if she would not make him indeed "monarch of all he surveyed;" and when all were once more in the carriages, he was seen on the piazza with his chair tilted back, and his feet *a la independent Virginian*, coolly muching the cake with which he had filled his pockets.

As they were about driving off, the owner of the place, a plain, bluff looking farmer, rode up on horseback, and the gentlemen of the party explained their unceremonious occupancy of his premises. With the ready hospitality of a native Georgian, he expressed pleasure that his house had been of use to them, and explained its vacancy by the fact that his servants were in the field, and he had been off to attend a church meeting.

"Behold the hero of your dreams," whispered the Historian to the girls—'I am sure he is a bachelor from the cut of his eye. Are you not afraid to leave your property so exposed?" he added aloud to the man.

"Oh no; this is an honest neighborhood," he replied, "and, besides, an old bachelor like myself is not generally supposed to have much to steal."

Amid the sly jokes and glances which this speech provoked, the ambulance drove off, followed by the other carriages. It soon began to rain so heavily that the gentlemen insisted upon putting all the ladies and children in the ambulance and carriage, and braving the inclemency of the weather in the open buggies.

The steepness of the hills told that they were approaching the mountain region, while the steamy breath and wet sides of the horses to the ambulance showed that they felt the change from the level roads to which they had been accustomed. The spirits of the party seemed to sink with the increasing gloom of the evening, till some one proposed some music to cheer them all up. After a few minutes consultation, several joined in a familiar air led by lady Montague's soft, clear soprano; Meg added a rich contralto, while Miss Patty proved that her voice was not so diminutive as her body, by furnishing a spirited alto, and the driver, Don Quixote, after some persuasion, supplied a mellow base; the rest were content to listen, and for miles grand anthems, and old fashioned hymns, such as might have resounded among the mountain fastnesses where the stern Covenanters held their meetings, kept time to the measured tramp of the horses' feet.

About five in the evening, the roofs and spires of Gainsville were seen in the distance, and there was a general rearranging of hair and dresses, so as to present as respectable an appearance as possible in passing through the town, which is the county seat of Hall, and contains a fine Court-House, a number of handsome residences, several churches, and a population of about four hundred souls. Its beauties were, however, lost upon the party, as they only passed through the suburbs, their only recollections being a long, muddy street with a row of small shops on one side, and on the other, a church yard, overgrown with grass so rank as to almost hide the discolored and broken tombstones that filled it.

The only moving thing to be seen in the street was a group of school children of various sizes, headed by a teacher so short, fair and fat, that he looked like a large roly poly dumpling, and was certainly a good walking advertisement of the feeding powers of the community—teachers and pastors being proverbialy as lean, lank and scrawny as their prototypes—church and academy mice.

It had been arranged that the party should spend the night with some friends living four miles from Gainsville, and they had hoped to find some member of the family in the village to guide them over the remainder of the road. In this, however, they were disappointed, but, as the rain had ceased, they determined to push on to their destination. Miss Patty Pace, who had passed over the road several times while making a visit to that part of the country in the early summer, was placed in the buggy with the Historian to guide the party, and they struck into the dense woods laying between Gainsville and the river.

Don Quixote, in the absence of the Historian, endeavored to give the party in the ambulance some outline of the country through which they were passing. He told them that they were now entering upon the mineral region of Georgia, that a half million dollars worth of gold had been found in Hale county alone, and several diamonds, one of which had been sold for two hundred dollars; while it was the opinion of scientific men who had investigated the subject, that large quantities of diamonds, besides iron, silver, lead, ruby, tourmaline, amethyst, emerald, granite and sandstone, would reward whoever had capital sufficient to sink the mines deep enough to reach them.

These statistics found very inattentive listeners, each one being intent upon finding the road, and watching the movements of the guides, who, being suspected of cherishing a *penchant* for each other, were the subjects of numberless jokes, as they rode along under the same umbrella, evidently well satisfied with themselves and their surroundings. A pause to adjust some part of the harness, gave our Artist a chance for another ludicrous caricature of "The Historian on a Dear Hunt," which went the rounds of the party, and served to keep up their drooping spirits for a time.

At length they came to a decided fork in the road, and Miss Patty, after a moment's thought, decided that the right hand road was the one to take, and they turned into it, though her hesitating manner had given general uneasiness to the party, for night was coming on rapidly, and a heavy cloud looming up in the west gave token that it would be one of storm. A dozen discontented voices begged the guides to pay more attention to the road, and less to each other; injunctions to which they paid little attention.

The harmony which had hitherto reigned in the ambulance, was now disturbed by Mrs. Gummidge, who having fallen into what Falstaff called one of her "low jingling ways," began to lament that they had ever undertaken the trip. The indignant remonstrances of her companions brought on a wordy war, which lasted until Miss Patty called back to say that she was afraid they had taken the wrong road, as she did not recognize anything around her.

The murmurs of discontent were "not loud, but deep," from all except Meg Merrilles, whose anger exploded in a quick flash of abuse at the stupidity of her cousin, Miss Patty, which was so vehement, and unlike her usual good humor, that it amused the whole party, and cleared up the vapors like a veritable electric current.

A fortunate cross-road relieved them of the dilemma of turning round in that dense forest, and brought them into the other track; but, as they were still uncertain about the route, it was decided that they would stop at the first house, if the wilderness in which they were involved could furnish one large enough to accommodate the party. As the horses began to show signs of great fatigue, even the roan drooping his usual lofty head, the ladies alighted and proceeded on foot; while it took all the skill of the gentlemen to guide the carriages over the miserable road.

At length the barking of dogs announced their approach to a house, and gave fresh alacrity to the steps of the walkers; but the relief was of short duration, for it turned out to be a log cabin situated in the midst of a collard patch, and giving but faint hopes of accommodation for the night. On interrogating the master of this domicil, he declined attempting to accommodate the party, butsaid they could easily reach their previous destination, though the Chattahoochee, only passable by means of a ferry-boat, intervened. He offered to guide them to the river, distant about half a mile, and they started ocne more, and soon reached the ferry, situated in the midst of low grounds over-grown with a heavy crop of carrot weeds, with no house in sight but the log cabin of the boatman situated on a distant hill on the opposite side of the river. When the gentlemen had exhausted their lungs with hallooing, two stout negro men were seen making their way through the weeds in the direction of the river, and after considerable delay, a large raft, used as a ferry-boat, was brought over, and the carriages carried over one by one.

Once more *en route*, the darkness began to descend rapidly accompanied by heavy rain. The road was miserable, and the rate of progress very slow. The first mishap was the jamming of a wheel against a tree, owing to the carelessness of a negro driver. After some difficulty, and any amount of hallooing, the obstacle was removed, and they started again. A few yards further, the foremost carriages were very near being precipatated over a precipice; general consternation prevailed, especially among the gentlemen, who were the only ones fully aware of the amount of damage they had escaped. At length the wished for haven came in view, and raised the spirits of the party, though considerable apprehension was felt as to the reception such a large party would receive at that late hour.

A cordial welcome soon put their doubts to flight, and after a plentiful supper, the party gladly retired to recruit their exhausted energies, and even the most mischievous of the girls was glad to go to sleep quietly; so silence soon reigned over the house.

CHAPTER VI.

The bright light of a cloudless morning found the entire party with renewed health and spirits, and ready for any scheme of amusement that might be proposed. After doing ample justice to their hostess' bountiful breakfast, a council of the elders was called, and it was decided to accept the cordial invitation of their entertainers and remain where they were till the next day, so as to give the horses a chance to rest before attempting the mountain roads that lay before them on the morrow.

The rest was as acceptable to man as beast, and it was a pleasant thing to be the guest of this old-fashioned farm house with its sloping roof, narrow halls and quaint rooms lighted by long windows with most diminutive panes placed far above the reach of the tallest person: all bearing the stamp of a past age, while the well cultivated fields, fertile orchards, and numberless barns and granaries told no tale of the neglect and decay which so frequently accompany antiquity. The master of the place was absent on business in another State, but his wife and her children dispensed the hospitalities of the house with a cordiality that made every one feel at home, and presented a pleasant picture of country life in Georgia among the better classes.

Lady Montague and her children went off to visit some relatives in the neighborhood, the other matrons and the young people gathered on the front porch to enjoy the beauty of the summer morning, and discuss the adventures of the previous day; and their blithe voices and merry laughter made the old house ring. The Historian, especially, seemed to imbibe elixir with every breath of morning air, and by his jokes and teasing soon had all the young ladies of the party arrayed against him, and eager to repay him in kind. Mrs. Gummidge alone took his part, and for some time was the only one that escaped a sarcasm that was too good-humored to offend even its victims, who one by one warned her that his complacency to her was only the playful gambols of a cat with a mouse that will yet suffer from its sharp claws.

The topic of to-morrow's journey was at length introduced, and he declared that he believed that they had reached the end of the road—that this was the jumping-off place—one step beyond which would land them all in nothingness—and their only mode of progression henceforth must be like that of the craw-fish—backwards.

"You remind me of a conversation I heard between two negroes in a show in Richmond during the war" said Don Quixote. "One was telling the other of a splendid farm he owned with trees on it seven hundred feet high, forty feet through the body and only one foot apart. Do you have any game down there?" enquired the other, who was quite a proper talking darkey. "We have a little game of seven up, sometimes." "Oh! I mean deer, rabbits, &c." "*Oh!* yes, lots of dat sort ov game. Deers forty feet from one tip of de horn to the other tip of de horn jest a tearing through de woods." "Well, now I think I have got you. You say the trees are seven hundred feet high, forty feet through the body, and stand only one foot apart; and the deer are forty feet from one tip of the horn to the other tip of the horn, and just a tearing through the woods." "Yes, sar, all dat just as true as preaching." "Well, now I want you to tell me how those deer got out of there?" "How dos deer git outer der? 'Taint any business ov mine how dey gits outer der," said the other, evidently non-plussed. "Yes, sir, you have got to tell me or I shall think you have been lying." "Well," scratching his head, and suddenly struck by a bright idea, "I'll tell you, dey gits out der like McClellan gits out de Chickahominy swamp—dey draws in der horns and backs out."

You think we will have to do the same Mr. Historian?

"I believe *I* will try McClellan's plan, and beat a retreat in the morning," he replied laughing. "And I am sure of having at least one companion in Mrs. Gummidge." "And thus show another attribute of the deer cloven foot," said Our Artist scornfully. "I wonder what has made you and Mrs. Gummidge so dissatisfied with the trip all at once? *She* has been grumbling ever since yesterday evening."

"I shall not attempt to explain the motives that influence *my* conduct, for none of you could appreciate them any more than you do the man; but I can easily tell you what is the matter with Mrs. Gummidge," he replied. "Her love affairs have not prospered as she expected they would. She has not been able to catch a *dear*."

This saucy hit, delivered in the very presence of one of the gentlemen for whom she had been accused of setting her cap, thoroughly discomfited his ally, and delighted the rest of the company, who kept up a running fire of raillery at her expense till the appearance of peaches, apples and sweet cider created a diversion.

While partaking of these refreshments, the ladies learned that a large pitcher of home-made wine which their hostess had sent up to them the night before as a preventive against cold, had been declared contraband of war, while passing through the gentlemen's room, and so much of it confiscated to their use that the servant was ashamed to carry the small quantity that remained to the ladies. Many vows of vengeance were uttered which they carried out by keeping their escorts awake nearly the whole of the next night.

The morning flew by rapidly, and, after doing justice to a fine dinner, the ladies slipped off one by one for their afternoon *siesta* from which they returned in an hour or two in fresh and bright afternoon toilets, which so excited the admiration of the gentlemen that there was a general call for valises and water in their room; and when they once more made their appearance below stairs, there was a decided improvement in the outer man, at least.

When the whole party, their hostess included, was once more settled on the shady porch, Aunt Quimby was requested to furnish her daily quota of entertainment from her memorandum book.

"I am more than usually willing to do so," she said with a smile, "because, as you already know, I have found in our hostess an old friend, who was my companion in many of these frolics, and can bear witness to their truth; so only asking that she will supply whatever I may have forgotten, I will proceed with my story, which I promise to make a short one.

THE GEORGIA WEDDING.

Mr. Carlton's place, which we reached that evening, was a lovely spot situated on the Chattahoochee. The house, with its vine-draped walls and lofty colonades, was placed on the top of a hill, so high as to almost merit its title of Ben Lomond; but which fell in gentle terraces to the river's bank, where a long bridge furnished means of communication with the factory and village situated on the opposite bank. The well-kept grounds and numerous out-buildings spoke of thrift and comfort, while the warm welcome of its inmates convinced the guest that Virginia hospitality had not been forgotten in a strange land. I found the family little changed, except in size. Mrs. Carlton being the same kind, motherly soul that I remembered in my childhood, while the years had passed so lightly over her head, that it was difficult to believe her the mother of two grown daughters; for May, the second daughter, was now sixteen, very tall for her age, and bidding fair to rival Meg in beauty.

Many quiet but pleasant days passed in assisting the family in the numberless preparations necessary for a large wedding; for Georgia house-keepers do not give a *carte blanche* to some confectioner for the furnishing of such entertainments, but, even the wealthiest, pride themselves on having everything prepared under their own supervision, and often produce master-pieces in the culinary art that would not shame a regular artiste. So, for days we lived in an atmosphere as redolent of sweets as that of Araby the Blest, till pantries and store-rooms were overflowing with cakes, looking like mounds of crystalized snow, amber jellies, golden fruits, and "lucent sirups tinct with cinnamon."

Two weeks before the wedding Mr. Lamar arrived, bringing with him his younger sister to spend the intervening time with us. I found Meg's betrothed a dignified, intelligent gentleman, for whom I formed a sincere friendship during his visit of three days. He left, promising to return the week before the wedding and bring with him the cousin with whom I was to stand, and upon whom I, of course, wished to make a favorable impression, as he was a young lawyer of considerable eminence.

Minnie Lamar was a gay sprite of a girl, very unlike the portly figure that now sits before me, smiling at the memory of those old days, when we churned syllabub, whipped custards, and frosted cakes together, and contrived to extract so much merriment from these homely operations, that Miss Juracy Cornell, the housekeeper, declared we were the "livliest and spryest gals it had ever been her fortin to meet." Poor Miss Juracy! her oddities, and the numberless tricks we played off on her, have been the occasion of many hearty laughs since.

The day before her brother was expected, Minnie threw down the paper horn with which she had been icing a last batch of cake and exclaimed: "If I taste or smell any more sweets, I am afraid some of the beaux may take me for a veritable sugar-plum, and devour me at the wedding. Do, Meg, let's go and take a long walk to bring back your roses, or you will pass that night for a monument erected to the memory of the late Meg Carlton."

But Meg was too busy putting the last touches to a dress to heed her chatter. Mrs. Carlton needed May, so she turned to me.

"Queenie, we'll have to be dignified all the time we are in Macon, and this is our last chance for a frolic before brother and all those tiresome men come; so let's have a good time.—Suppose we dress up as beggar-women and pay the "factory folks" a visit.

I agreed, for in those days I was always ready for anything that promised fun, and we hunted up all ahe old garments that we could find, and arrayed ourselves in them, amid the laughter of the children and servants. We were grotesque figures when our toilets were completed. Minnie wore an old black dress of Mrs. Carlton's, without crinoline, a red plaid shawl, black calico sun bonnet, and blue cotton gloves. I was equally as ludicrous in a blue and yellow plaid homespun, borrowed from Miss Juracy, which was immensely large in the waist, and so long and tight in the skirt that I could scarcely step, My hair was twisted after the most approved factory fashion, in a tight roll at the back of each ear, while one of the boys' broad brimmed straw hats was tied under my chin with a red silk handkerchief.

Thus equipped we sallied forth, and, entering the village, stopped at every house, sometimes asking for bread, at others permission to stay all night. Nobody recognized us, but all refused to entertain such suspicious looking characters; and, after having as much fun as we wanted, we strolled off up the river to look for holly and mistletoe to finish the decorations of the parlor. Here, in attempting to jump a muddy ditch, I fell in, dragging Minnie with me, and as soon as we could extricate ourselves from the mud, we scampered home to change our wet clothes. We were creeping in slyly by the back way to keep Mr. Carlton from seeing us, when a young gentleman suddenly stepped from behind one of the pillars of the colonade, and catching Minnie in his arms, pressed his moustached lips to hers. The shriek she gave, so alarmed me that I became entangled in my wet dress and rolled down the steps, to be picked up by a strikingly handsome young man who was returning from the stables with Mr. Lamar. He placed me on my feet, and there I stood, ready to sink into the earth with mortification; for my hat had fallen off in the tumble, and I felt his keen eyes scanning my blushing face, and taking in every detail of my absurd dress. Mr. Lamar, who was a little behind, took in the situation at glance, and without pausing, said carelessly in the tone he would use to a servant, "You should be a little more careful, Martha," and passed on with his companion into the house.

Minnie, in the meantime, had made her escape unnoticed, after discovering that the supposed young gentleman was

May Carlton who had dressed up in her father's clothes to frighten us; and on reaching our room, I found them both in convulsions of laughter at the impression I must have made on Herbert Lindsay. In spite of my vexation, I could not help joining in their merriment, and it was some time before Meg could sober us enough to prepare to entertain the gentlemen who had arrived in our absence.

I made a careful toilet and descended, hoping that Mr. Lindsay might not recognize in the stately young lady in fashionable attire, the scarecrow whom he had probably taken for a mulatto girl. There was no sign of recognition as he bowed with courtly grace at the mention of my name, though once or twice during the evening I detected a gleam of amusement in his dark eyes as they rested on me, that made me fear he was recalling the *contretemp* of our meeting. In spite of this uneasiness, the evening passed pleasantly, and I formed a very favorable impression of the gentlemen who were to act as groomsmen.

They were staying with a friend in the neighborhood, and were to accompany the groom on the morrow to the county town, distant about twenty miles, to procure his license, and would not return till the day before the wedding, so that I saw nothing more of Herbert Lindsay, till we met to take our places in the bridal train.

The attendants were eight in number; the ladies being Minnie, May, Carrie Lindsay, and myself. By Meg's request, I was first bridesmaid, and upon me devolved much of the duty of entertaining the large company that began to assemble by dark, and comprised the best people of the neighborhood, as well as many strangers from Athens and Macon, in which latter city, the Lamars resided. The ceremony had gone off *en regle*, the bride had blushed and cried in the most approved manner without making her nose or eyes red, and with her attendants around her was standing near the centre of the room, conversing with a large group of her husband's city relatives. Conscious of looking my very best in my vapory white crepe and pearl ornaments, I was dividing my attention between several distinguished gentlemen who had solicited introductions, when, happening to raise my eyes, I saw Ike Thigpen's long chin hooked over the shoulder of a gentleman before me, coolly staring down into my face.

My first impulse was to turn my back on him; but, as soon as he caught my eye, he elbowed his way through the group, and, extending a hand that looked like a joint of uncooked meat, exclaimed in a loud, rasping voice that attracted the attention of all around us:—"Well Miss Quimby! I'm powerful tickled to see you agin. You see we hern Miss Magrat was going to marry, so sister Civilia Bernice and me, thought we'd come up to see her hitched."

Sure enough, just behind him loomed Miss Civilia in the identical costume already described; while Ike was decked in a swallow tailed blue coat with brass buttons, a flaming red vest, butternut pants, and a stove pipe hat set on the back of his head which he could not be persuaded to remove.

It cost me a short, but sharp, mental struggle to brave the wondering eyes around me, and acknowledged my acquaintance with this grotesque pair, for I had all the sensitiveness in regard to appearances common to my youthful years; but I shook hands with both, and, while they paid their respects to the bride, I slipped away, I thought unobserved, till, as I reached the door of tho parlor, Herbert Lindsay's voice sounded at my side asking me to accept his arm for a promenade.—He led me out on the colonade, and walked up and down in silence till my burning cheeks cooled; then with gentle tact led me to talk other things, and I soon forgot my mortification in the charm of his conversation.

Only once more during the evening did Ike approach me, and then it was to ask me to "pull some music out of that ar red box"—meaning the piano. I was about to refuse, but Meg whispered to me to gratify him, and I complied by playing some of my livliest pieces. Ike stood by in open-mouth wonder for awhile, but suddenly startled the whole company by exclaiming, "Lor sakes, the gal haint got no jints in her fingers."

This speech ended the music abruptly, and I saw nothing more of Ike till at the supper table I heard him request Herbert Lindsay to hand him "a sasser of that frozen butter what the cows give when they run in the sweet grass bed."

Herbert's looks, as he handed him the ice cream, which a fortunate freeze had enabled us to have, entirely upset my gravity, and, catching my eye, we indulged in a hearty laugh, and as Ike moved away I was able to explain to him the circumstances of my acquaintance with this oddity, after which we amused ourselves by watching him.

He had forced himself up next to the bridal party, and Minnie, who was a very imp of mischief, saw in him fine sport, and began a conversation by asking him how he liked the ice-cream.

"Well, its purty good, but just about the coldest thing I ever put down my goozle," he replied.

Seeing her give her partner a small cake with a name on it, he inquired what it was, and she told him she had given the gentleman a heart with his lady love's name on it, and showed him a plate of similar ones.

"Lor sakes. I wonder if thar's any chance of my finding *my* sweetheart's name thar," he said.

"Tell me what her name is, and I will look," she answered.

"I'm scared she might hear me," he said with a foolish grin.

"Oh is she here?" she exclaimed. "Then just tell me her initials."

"Well her initials is, *Quimby.*"

Minnie comprehended in a minute, and almost convulsed with delight at the joke she had on me, selected a cake with my name on it, and presented it to Ike who grinned from ear to ear.

Even my position in the bridal train could not keep me in that spot any longer, and I took particular pains to keep out of the way of the Thigpens for the remainder of the evening.

Most of the guests from a distance remained all night, and at the breakfast table the next morning, Mr. Carlton, instigated by Minnie, told of my conquest, and I had to run a perfect gauntlet of raillery, which I bore as best I might, though very much annoyed.

There was to be a reception during the morning. Herbert Lindsay and several other gentlemen had told me they intended to call, and about eleven o'clock I was descending the stairs after a careful toilet, when I heard Ike Thigpen's voice in the porch asking if I was at home.

Determined not to see him, I flew down the back-stairs, through the garden, and, knowing Minnie would leave no place about the house unsearched, I took refuge in an empty corn crib, crouching down in the darkest corner careless of my rich silk and handsome laces. There I remained till my watch told me the dinner hour was passed; then, creeping round by the kitchen, I learned that my "Bubly Jock" was gone, and ventured into the dining room to beg Miss Juracy to give me some dinner. I found Mrs. Carlton still there, and she told me that Ike, after sitting in the parlor some time looking like a fish out of water, asked, "If Miss Quimby was at home, that he had a few things to say to her."

Mr. Carlton and Minnie, eager for fun, had searched the place for me, but without success, and Ike had finally taken his leave. I was telling her my hiding-place, when Mr. Carlton came in to light his pipe, and the fuss he made over the "runaway" soon called every one else in, and the fun at my expense, "waxed fast and furious," till Mrs. Carlton, taking compassion on me, drove them all out so that I could finish my dinner in peace.

My discomfiture was complete, when I learned that the gentleman had called in my absence, and, with many regrets at not seeing me, had taken their departure for their homes in Athens. Nothing was to be done, however, but let my vexation evaporate, in that woman's solace, a good cry, which I indulged in under the pretence of taking a nap.

The next day the bridal train started for Macon, and among the refined and cultivated people I met there, I learned to properly appreciate Georgia character, and to know that the Thigpens were exceptions. I never saw Ikey again, but the nickname he had given me followed me back to Virginia, and is still my familiar appellation among my friends; while my little nieces and nephews do not know that I have any other name than "Aunt Quimby;" and so ends my story.

"Queenie said I must supply whatever she omitted," said our hostess, as Aunt Quimby left the porch to put away her memorandum book. "She has left out the romance of the story because it concerned herself. My cousin Herbert fell a victim to her charms in spite of the untoward fate that ruled their early acquaintance. He visited her frequently while she remained in Georgia, and they were engaged when she returned to Virginia. What broke it off, I never knew, though I have always suspected that May Carlton had a large share in the affair, for Herbet married her several years afterwards, though he once said to me, that, in spite of misunderstandings, Queenie must ever remain his ideal of a perfect woman. He is now a widower, and the start Queenie gave last night when I told her, made me hope that their difficulty might yet be explained satisfactorily. Time only can prove; meanwhile you will not thank me for sitting here talking sentiment, and neglecting your suppers," and she hastened away, jingling her key basket, leaving the rest to comment, at their leisure, upon this glimpse into Aunt Quimby's history.

CHAPTER VII.

The next morning found the party, with the addition of a portion of their hostess' family, again on the road. For hours they threaded the dense forest covering that part of Hall county, catching now and then, through the vail of leaves, fleeting glimpses of the Chattahoochee, rushing and tumbling over the dams that impede its course; but ere long they bade farewell for that day to the silvery gleam of its waters, and began to ascend mountain sides so steep that it required the full power of the horses to draw the vehicles. The road still continued bad, though one forgave the roughness for the beauty of the spots through which it passed. Soon the face of the country put on a wild and fantastic appearance as the elevated spurs of the Blue Ridge began to rise above the horizon; some, bold, craggy and preciptious, lifting their naked heads towards the sky, as if defying the wrath of the elements; others, clothed with a natural tapestry of leafy green, and sloping with an almost imperceptible declivity to the general level of the land; while in the far distance Mt. Yonah, meaning in the Cherokee tongue the Great Bear, kept guard over the realm of lesser mountains.

Some one has said that the grading of roads with the consequent destruction of surrounding beauties, disfigures a country, and prevents its pleasing features from being viewed save at a distance. If this be the case, it should be the fervent wish of every true lover of nature that it may be many years ere the utilitarian spirit of Mac Adam visits the country of which I am writing; for the roads in use there now, however rough, have the merit of bringing the traveler in close companionship with surrounding beauties. They lead him over hills where he may catch magnificent views of mountain peaks and fertile valleys outspread into a wide surface of checkered green, now dark, now light, and fading so gently into the dim distance far away, that you can almost believe it a world of waters that bounds your vision. Then they dip suddenly into deep dells where merry brooklets, shaded by sycamores, water-birch, and sugar maples, gather their tricklings, cool and clear as crystal, from the surrounding mountains; or, seized with a social fit, take their course through farm yards, or by cabin doors, whose inmates pause from their homely domestic tasks to gaze at you with eager interest, or proffer with ready kindness, the products of their dairies and orchards, the only wealth which they possess. But so rare are these signs of civilization, so solitary the roads, and dense the wooded growth that one could almost cheat themselves with the belief that they were journeying in primeval days, and might expect to hear the solitudes around them re-echo with the war-whoop of the brave Cherokee, or Choctaw, or catch through the interstices of the leafy curtain that vails their way, glimpses of the wigwams of "deer skins bleached and whitened."

As the sole motives of the party was enjoyment, and there was no impatience to reach their journey's end, their course was eratic, bearing much resemblance to that which in childish fable was said to lead to Robin Hood's barn, in its old-fashioned attributes of time, distance, and beguiling incidents. They rode, walked, laughed, sung and talked, gathered wild berries, rested themselves upon moss, logs, or shaded rocks, ate their lunch under embowering vines amid fertile orchards, drank deep draughts from clear, cold springs, and filled the long, bright day, with the pure elixir of youthful pleasures, the evanescent sparkle of which is as difficult to portray by pen and paper as to imprison the aroma of the golden vintage.— Nor is it possible in the brief space to which this book is limited, to mention half the incidents, which, however amusing in the occurrence, might prove "flat, stale and unprofitable" to the reader; so that a general outline of the principal places and events is all that can be attempted.

About noon the tourists passed from Hall into White, a newly established county, formed from portions of Hall, Habersham and Rabun; and about night reached the village of Cleveland, formerly callled Mt. Yonah. It is a small place, containing one church, one school, three stores, and a blacksmith's shop, and chiefly remarkable for the magnificence of the mountain scenery around it, and its proximity to Cedar Springs, whose medicinal qualities have lately been discovered, and, are said to be as remarkable as that of the Pool of Siloam; insomuch as they make the blind to see, the lame to walk, the leper to be cleansed; and prove such a "fountain of youth" to the aged, that in spite of the want of accommodation a crowd of "impotent folk" gather there every season. Such was the account given the writer by a voluble lady who had spent some weeks in a cabin on the spot.

The single hotel of Cleveland looked so unpromising that the party passed through without stopping, and decided to camp in a beautiful grove surrounding an old church in the outskirts of the village; and to allow the ladies to make use of the tents, as the night promised to be warm and cloudless. They were delighted with this new feature of Bohemian life, and hastened to make their preparations for the night, unheeding the cynical smiles exchanged among the gentlemen at their expressions of delight at the prospect of sleeping with only "the calm blue sky above, the grassy sward beneath them."

While a portion of the party attended to the horses, those of the gentlemen who were supposed to be most familiar with camp life from their experience as soldiers, were called upon to erect the two tents, which the ladies had prepared before leaving home. But they soon found that the proportions of either were entirely too small for the number to be accommodated; and, after a great deal of trouble and discussion, they succeeded in making of the two, one rather rickety affair, that might cover the ladies and children by close packing, while the gentlemen would sleep on their blankets under the adjacent trees as a body guard.

These preparations being completed, and a fire kindled, the matrons and servants set about preparing supper, while the young people, attracted by the beauty of the scenery around them, strolled of in various directions. A party seated themselves on the steps of the church, and there Rashleigh Obaldiston, who had been remarkably quiet throughout the journey, distinguished himself by taking a seat too near a yellow-jacket's nest. The infuriated insects suddenly surrounded his head, and he began to fight, stamp, and call upon one of the young ladies to rescue him, to the no small amusement of the whole party; and, as short as the step between the sublime and the ridiculous is said to be, it is far more difficult in the ascent than the descent, so it was many minutes before the risibles of the company became sufficiently composed to pay attention to the glories of the sunset unrolled before them. It was indeed, a lovely vision of the gate of evening, framed in by the strong buttresses of the mountains, and guarded by one solitary sentry, the evening star; while within the unbarred portals you caught glimpses in the distance of domes of gold, mighty pillars, and high arched roof spangled and veined with amber, pearl and amethyst; and surrounded by lands fair as those of Beulah, overarched by fadeless rainbows and opal tinted skies, sweet and peaceful as the spirits of the wearied saints who there find perfect rest unto their souls: all illuminated as from below the horizon by an imprisioned radiance, seemingly the very essence of the sun, whose disc had already disappeared.

The wondrous beauty of the scene crept into the hearts of even these gay observers. Nature spoke to them with her "still, small voice," and there was a deep stillness only broken at length by the voice of Aunt Quimby, repeating solemnly:—"Is not God in the height of heaven? He holdeth back the face of his throne, and spreadeth his cloud upon? He bindeth the sweet influence of the Pleiades, and looseth the bonds of Orion. Lo these are parts of His ways, but the thunders of his powers who can understand?"

"Why is it," asked the Historian, as the georgeous pageant faded before the cool shades of evening, "that in viewing any great exhibition of Nature's works, we feel so plainly the barrenness of our common language to express what we feel, and instinctively fall back upon the grand words of the Bible? I have no doubt each one was thinking of some passage similar to those Aunt Quimby repeated."

"Because only the mind that originated these grand works, could frame language suitable to describe them," said the Artist. But I assure you, you must not think we are all such "sky-scrapers" as you and Aunt Quimby. *I* was thinking that mountain sunsets would be glorious things transferred to canvas, if the *cadmium* with which they have to be painted was not *so* expensive."

The gravity with which this utilitarian idea was advanced, was so ludicrous that a hearty laugh restored them all to their natural level, and they descended the hill to meet the walkers and enquire into their adventures. They found them disposed to grumble terribly at the lack of supplies in the village, which they had visited in search of crackers, cheese, and fresh eggs, or any other eatables to add to their store; as well as of the rudeness of the male inhabitants, which had seriously alarmed the ladies, whose nerves were so unstrung that on going up to the old church in search of seats they become so alarmed that their screams brought the gentlemen to their assistance, and they found they had been frightened by their own shadows reflected in the moonlight which streamed through the windows.

These alarms were, however, forgotten when they gathered around the long table, that the church had supplied, to partake of supper, which the matrons in vain tried to limit to bread, butter, fruit and coffee. There was a general out-cry for meat, which Falstaff said reminded him of the Icelandic fable, which he proceeded to relate while waiting for his coffee to cool. "A man, named Fusi, seated himself one Christmas-eve at a cross road, to wait for the elves who come at this time with their riches. It is only necessary not to speak to them, or take anything from during the whole night, otherwise they will vanish, and all their riches are turned into stones. But when the sun rises, one must say: "God be praised, now it is morning in the heavens," and the elves vanish, leaving their stores behind them. Fusi, then, was sitting by the cross-road, and an elf came to him, and asked him if he would not partake of a piece of fat. The temptation was too great to be resisted, and he replied. 'Fat have I never refused!' But alas! fat, elf, and all vanished from his sight.

In return for this story, he was allowed to have a *bonne bouche* of the coveted fat, and the others profited by his indulgence, and helped themselves. When the meal was at length over, the matrons and children retired to the tent, but the young people lingered around the fire, lured by the novelty of their surroundings.

The slender crescent of the young moon had already sunk out of sight behind the mountains, but its place was supplied by myriads of stars that peeped through every opening in the leafy screen above their heads, and though they afforded but little help to the camp-fire in routing the shadows that lingered out-side of the circle of light in sufficient force to inspire in the timid hearts of the ladies that inseparable adjunct of darkness—danger—and give the gentlemen a pleasant feeling of protection towards their fair companions. The sighing of the night wind in the heavy branches of the trees, an occasional snort from the horses tethered on the opposite side of the road, the distant and plaintive cry of the whippoorwill, mingled with, but did not disturb the low hum of conversation around the fire. Don Quixote regretted the absense of music which might lend its witching strains to the soft influence of the hour, whose memory he could never forget; but as this gallant speech was made while in the unromantic employment of holding a long bar of rosin soap with which Miss Patty Pace was washing out some pocket-handkerchiefs, its effect was somewhat impaired by a pertinent question from Meg, as to which would occupy the most prominent place in his rememrance—love or soap.

The fun which this excited, lasted till some of the elders, pointing to the rapid march of certain familiar constellations towards the zenith, warned the others the "wee sma hours" were approaching, and with many good nights, and wishes for pleasant dreams the ladies set out for the tent.

A rather unpromising prospect for sleep was revealed by the lifting of the flap that answered for a door. The tent, a mere fly thrown over a ridge-pole, did not cover an extent of more than fourteen square feet of ground; upon this had been loosely thrown the oats and fodder designed for the forage of the horses on the morrow, and covered by all the bed clothes of the party. In the centre of this unique bed were disposed the three matrons and the seven children in attitudes more comfortable, than graceful, leaving only a circular strip, about a foot wide, round the edges, for the accommodation of the seven young ladies.

After a prolonged survey of this contracted space, Die Vernon declared that she for the first time realized the utility of the Grecian Bend; for, whoever was most afflicted with it, could best accommodate themselves to the position they all had to occupy during the night, that of a circular hedge to a young vineyard; and, having thus expressed her opinion, she and Meg seized the one small piece of candle, and went off to the wagon to overhaul the trunk that contained "the wardrobe of the troupe," for some clean collars for the morning's adornment.

The others, being left in darkness to make their preparations for the night, soon awakened the sleepers by their unwary stumblings, and a scene of disturbance ensued, mingled with dismal calls for light, which were answered by one of the gentlemen thrusting a lighted candle under one edge of the tent in such close proximity to some of the party as to produce such a general stampede to the other side, as was very near knocking down the frail supports of the tent. Amid the "confusion worse confounded," which now reigned in this cloth habitation, it was a proof of the amiability of the party that nobody lost her temper, but every mishap provoked fresh amusement.

At last by dint of pushing, squeezing, and skillful adaptation of themselves to corners, as well as circumstances, every one found a resting place for their bodies, and were agreeing to be satisfied with this, when the appearance of Mrs. Page with a bottle of brandy and honey in one hand, and one of Plantation Bitters in the other, renewed the fun. She had provided these medicines in case of snake-bites, and now declaring that it was equally necessary to protect them from cold, insisted upon each one taking a swallow. The change of posture necessary to the accomplishment of this, was not made without noise, which was at its hight when loud shouts in the direction of the village attracted their attention. In a moment all was still as death, every sense being concentrated in that of listening. It was soon ascertained that they were drunken shouts and rapidly approaching nearer. The wildest fear took possession of them, as tales of the lawlessness of White county rushed upon their memories. In vain the most collected strove to reassure the others by representing the well-known bravery of the gentlemen, and their power to protect them. Their confidence in their male protectors weakened with their distance from them, and when some one whispered that the only two pistols in the company belonged to the negro drivers, the panic reached its hight. Some began to replace the few articles of dress they had laid aside, preparatory to hasty flight, they knew not where; others sat helplessly weeping and trembling in the darkness, afraid to speak or move.

A few moments of intense anxiety passed, then the voices of the gentlemen were heard in the vicinity of the tent. They had ascertained that the noise proceeded from some drunken revelers passing along the road to their homes without a thought of molesting them; and had returned to reassure the ladies, and tell them they might sleep in peace for they would lie under the neighboring trees and keep guard. The revulsion of feeling which these words produced was so great that Meg declared that they could all sleep the balance of the night on a bed of augers, beset by a tribe of the lo gad-flies of which St. Elmo talked; but she soon found herself mistaken, for they were scarcely settled again, when it was discovered that the fire having been built in a hog-bed, the fleas had been driven down the hill into the tent, and with a swarm of black ants that had their nest in a hollow in the tree against which the tent was placed, threatened to expel the human inhabitants.

Very disturbed slumbers were the consequence. nor did the gentlemen fare much better, if one might judge from their groans and frequent exclamations; and, late in the night, convulsions of laughter from Falstaff that seemed to shake the ground, provoked by the solemn adjuration of Roscius to the vermin not to make a meal of him before he was under the sod.

CHAPTER VIII.

The first gleam of day found them all willing to leave their uncomfortable couches, and Meg and Cap, the most elastic natures in the company, declaring they felt fully as much in need of "shaking up" as the Smallweeds of Bleak House memory, started off to look for a flowing brook in which to make their ablutions; and returned after sometime, with cheeks that had been painted by the rosy fingers of the morning, to laugh at the generally haggard and uncomfortable look of the others yawning over their unpalatable breakfast of cold bread and meat, while they parried with what skill they could the laughing banter of the gentlemen on their partiality for *camp* life.

It had been arranged that they should make the ascent of Mt. Yonah, three miles distant, so dispatch was the order of the day until they were once more in the carriages and leaving Cleveland behind them.

It was a fresh, breezy morning; brilliant flashes of sunlight alternating with deep shadows, making of the land-scape a series of pictures, each different, yet all so abounding in beauty, that a painter would have lingered with delight over their effects of light and shade, glorious displays of color, and graceful groupings of dark woods, open fields and rugged mountains. Early morning among the mountains has a charm for the imaginative mind unknown to any other time of the day; and that, even the elders of this party were true lovers of nature, might be seen from the readiness with which they forgot the discomforts of the night in the sweet influences of the hour. The fast flitting clouds, the breezy grass, the rich odors of wild flowers that rose from the banks of the dancing brooklets, the mellow whistle and gorgeous hues of the red birds that fluttered through the thickets that bordered the road; all were enjoyed with the keen zest of children.

They were now on the borders of the Cherokee country, and the practiced eye would at once notice a change in the geological formations of the land; and detect the presence of limestone in the luxuriant growth of small grain and grasses. The constitution of the soil and the rock formations being similar to those of the Genesee Valley in New York, and the Shenandoah in Virginia, the time may yet come when the wilderness may blossom like the rose; and this portion of Georgia may be as remarkable for its *agricultural*, as it is now for its *mineral* wealth, and abundant water power. The general soil is good; with proper care all kinds of grass grow luxuriantly, and the whole country is peculiarly adapted to grazing. Corn, wheat, rye, oats, barley and buckwheat, reward the farmer with fine crops; while the orchard products are remarkably abundant, and the forests are rich in oak, chestnut, walnut, beech, white pine, spruce and hemlock. The climate is very pure and healthy, the scenery unrivalled in beauty; and, when its agricultural and mineral wealth shall be developed, the North East portion of the State will become the garden-spot of Georgia. That the Air-Line Railroad will prove the open sesame which will unlock these hidden treasures, few can doubt who have ever traveled through this section.

The course of the travelers lay through the narrow belt of elastic sandstone which runs from Hog mountain in Hall county to Habersham in the N. E. corner of the State. This strata is the home of the diamond, some dozen having been already found; and, in 1828, the discovery of gold both in vein and deposit, threw the people of this region into great excitement, which gradually extended itself to the adjoining State, even Calhoune falling a victim to the epidemic, and proving how poor a match great learning is for practical cunning, by paying ten thousand dollars for a mine not worth as many hundreds. In this instance he fell a victim to the well known practice of "salting," or transferring gold by slight-of-hand to the pans while washing; but he afterwards purchased a vein where the gold was imbedded in a strata of rock which proved of immense value.

How the rich quartose veins, or alluvial materials that compose the deposit mines are formed, is a question best left to the geologist; but it is now well known, that, though the mining fever has in a great measure subsided, there is more gold in this region than there ever was in all the bank vaults in the United States, and that a pit can scarcely be sunk in these hills and valleys without finding particles of the precious metal. For this reason, proprietors sell with great reluctance even at fifty dollars per acre, as a small lot may contain a mine worth thousands of dollars. The Nacoochee Hydraulic Mining Company was established just before the late war by New England enterprise. It has now in possession, either by lease or purchase, eight thousand acres of the best mining ground in Georgia, which is washed by a canal twelve miles in length that cost forty thousand dollars. They work on the California system with improved machinery, and there seems to be no reason why fortunes should not be more easily realized here, than in that ElDorado of the West, as fissure veins, such as exist in these mountains, always improve in size and quality. Very little, however, did the gay party traversing this country think of the hidden riches beneath their feet, for the present, at least, their thoughts were not of "the earth earthy," but were soaring to the top of the tall peak that arose before them in solemn grandeur, presenting on the side next to them a perpendicular wall of grey free-stone more than a thousand feet in hight, from the summit of which, in fair weather, a magnificent view of the surrounding country can be obtained. The ascent could only be made on foot from the other side of the mountain, and all were eager to attempt it; but, on reaching the nearest practicable point for the carriages, it was found that the clouds had suddenly become so dark and lowering as to promise only a thorough wetting in payment for the toil of climbing, so the ascent was abandoned, and they turned reluctantly away. But they were soon repaid for their disappointment by their entrance into Nacoochee Valley, the beauties of which far exceeded their already exalted anticipations, and of which words, however fitly chosen, can give but a faint idea.

Imagine an ellipsis eight miles in length and half a mile wide, encircled on every side by mountains; of which Mt. Yonah, the tallest peak, stands sentinel at the entrance. From the north-west come the Chattahoochee dashing down from its head-springs among the Blue Ridge, and, forgetting here the Indian significance of its name, "Flowered Rocks," flows on through beautiful lowlands, and disappears between two abrupt mountain peaks.

The graphic words used in describing a valley in another State, rush upon the mind in entering this, which might easily pass for the original of the "Happy Valley" described. The writer says: "Everything which can enrich and delight has been lavished here in bounteous profusion. Here are green meadows and wide grazing pastures. Here are oaks, cedars, pines, the spruce, the silver, the white, and the black; walnuts, poplars, locusts, chestnuts, hollies, and the white and pink blossomed laurels. Here are pure, gushing springs, and noisy, babbling rills, which dash down from the mountain-tops, as if in haste to bury themselves in the vasty deep. Here are freshing fogs, which rise not from malaria, but from pure streams, bearing on their downy pinions the glittering dew-drops and the rose of health, and not disease and death. Here are bracing breezes and cool nights, which strengthen man for the duties and toil of the long summer days. Here are fishes, sweet-singing birds, and deer; and here are groves not inferior to that of Daphne by Orentes."

"Wild luxurauce—generous tillage,—
Here alternate meet the view;
Every turn, through all thy windings,
Still revialing something new."

The entire valley of Nacoochee is owned by several brothers of the name of Williams, whose father made large purchases there when that portion of Georgia was a wilderness country, mainly inhabited by Indians. Charmed with the rich lands, pure air and water, and magnificent mountain scenery, his sons as they grew up, settled around the old homestead, and the entire valley is now owned by them. There are three residences in sight of each other, and Mr. G. W. Williams of Charleston has lately bought an extensive estate at the upper end of the valley, upon which he intends erecting an elegant summer residence. A competent land-scape gardener will be employed to make the grounds a Central Park in miniature, and when Art thus lends a helping hand to Nature it must be a Momus indeed that can find fault with this lovely spot.

In 1834 some miners while excavating a canal discovered the remains of an Indian town at a distance of from seven to nine feet from the surface, inbedded in gravel. The houses, thirty-four in number, were built of logs from six to ten inches in diameter, and from ten to twelve feet in length. Specimens of curious workmanship, cane baskets and fragments of earthenware were found in the rooms, leaving little doubt that it was an Indian village, overwhelmed by the outbreak of some mountain torrent, carrying with it the stratum of auriferous gravel in which the houses are found imbedded; for the perishable character of the schistose rocks which compose these mountains, renders them pecnliarly liable to the action of water, as has been demonstrated by the mining operations now in progress there. The mountain slide which buried this village must have occurred many centuries ago, as the spot was covered when the whites first settled the country, by a heavy growth of timber, which denoted the great antiquity of the catastrophe; and the ruins are probably those of Nacoochee, Old Town, said to have been visited by the Spaniards as early as the twelfth century, in search of gold and diamonds.

In later years, Nacoochee, the largest town of the Cherokee Nation, stood near the centre of this valley, strongly defended by fortifications which extended across the valley from mountain to mountain. Along the lines of these fortifications, mounds were raised on which Indian chiefs resided in their mud-thatched palaces. Not a vestage of the town now remains. The once strong walls of Nacoochee are leveled to the ground, and but one single mound remains to tell the traveler that Indians once possessed this beautiful country, to which they must look back from the distant west as Adam did upon a lost Eden.

"Where oh! graceful NACOCHEE
  Are the warriors who of old
Sought thee, at thy mountain sources,
  Where thy springs are icy cold—
Gone forever from thy borders,
  But immortal in thy name,
Are the red men of the forest!—
  Be thou keeper of their fame!
Paler races dwell upon thee,
  Celt and Saxon till thy lands,
Wedding use unto thy beauty,—
  Linking over thee their hands."*

The party found in Col. E. P. Williams at whose house they stopped for a short rest, a most kind and obliging host, and several hours were whiled away most pleasantly in listening to his account of the valley, and trying to transfer to paper the beauties around them.

Some one has advanced the idea that there are lovlier pictures on canvas than are found in Nature. This may be true where the human face is concerned, for no living countenance ever yet bore the stamp of divinity, as plainly as it may glow beneath the pencil; but such is not the case with the works

* These verses were written of the Swannona River of N. C.

upon which God has set the seal of his power. Where is the artist that can paint truly the sun as a world of light illuminating the universe, or find "colors of such divinity" as to paint "the bended bow upon the heavens?" So among the beauties of Nacoochee, the mind wonders, adores, and places its scenes among the fairest in memory's gallery, but no pencil has yet been found that could paint the dissolving views of such a landscape, ever varying, ever changing. Nor can the photographic art produce a picture that will equal the original, from the impossibility of obtaining such a position as will take in the most striking objects in the world of mountains that there opens upon the sight.

In spite of the dark cloud that rested upon Mt. Yonah, the sure precurser of a storm before night, it was with considerable difficulty that the gentlemen at length succeeded in persuading the ladies to re-enter the carraiges, so much were they delighted with their surroundings. Then many a backward glance told that they had no fear of the fate of Lot's wife before their eyes. Long after they left the valley, every backward glance took in the grand proportions of Mt. Yonah, and Mrs. Gummidge repeated softly Ruskin's grand description of the crest of the Alps:—"The child looks up to it in the dawn, and the husbandman in the burden and heat of the day, and the old man in the going down of the sun, and it is to them all as the celestial city on the world's horizon; dyed with the depth of Heaven and clothed with the calm of eternity. There was it set for holy dominion by Him who marked for the sun his journey, and bade the moon know her going down."

"Let me give you a companion picture of American birth, addressed to a mountain of your own State," said Our Artist, "but I think equally applicable to Mt. Yonah:"—"It satisfies the eye, and fills the soul with a calm and solemn delight.—Whether touched by the fleecy clouds of morning, or piercing the glittering skies of noon, or reposing in the mellow tints of evening; whether bathed in the pale light of the moon, or enveloped in the surges of the tempest, with the lightning flashing around its brow, it stands ever, ever the same; its foundations in the depths of the earth, and its summit rising in solitary grandeur to the heavens, just as it rose under its Maker's hand, on the morning of creation, and just as it shall stand when the last generation shall gaze upon it for the last time."

"I, too, have a mite to add that may increase your interest in Nacoochee and Mt. Yonah," said the Historian, producing his note book. "Mr. Williams was kind enough to furnish me with some traditions of the Valley written by himself, and I copied them *verbatim*. You all noticed the blasted pine that stood on the top of the mound? During the war it bore aloft the Confederate flag, but died with our lost cause. It is centuries old, and was placed there to mark the grave of Nacoochee, the Cherokee Evening Star, from whom the valley takes its name, and this is the legend: "Nacoochee was the only daughter of a noted Cherokee chief. She possed remarkable beauty and grace of manners. This lovely maid of the valley was woed by many a gallant youth; but, unfortunately, was won by a brave young warrior of the Choctaw Nation, a tribe at that time bitter enemies of the Cherokees, and frequently engaged in fierce warfare with them."

One dark night Nachoochee disappeared from her vine-clad wigwam. She had eloped with Sautee, son of a Choctaw chief. The father of Nacoochee summoned a hundred stout warriors to go in pursuit of his erring daughter. The valleys and mountains echoed the terrific war-whoop, as they were searching every hill and dale.

Days and nights passed, but Sautee and the bright-eyed Indian girl could nowhere be found. The enraged father refused to eat or sleep. He believed the lovers had sought refuge under the Great Bear (Yonah) of the valley. Renewed and more diligent search was made. Sautee had selected a bridal chamber for his young princess amid the rocky fastnesses of Mt. Yonah, which was amply supplied with venison and wild turkey. He regarded the rugged cliffs rising in their native grandeur, as secure from the intrusion of friend or foe. Nacoochee's new home must have been a second Eden; before her stood a world of mountains, rising one above another until their lofty peaks were lost in the blue sky; while at her feet nestled the lovely valley of Nacoochee and Sautee, covered with fragrant flowering trees, and brilliant rhododendrons and azalias. From the crevices in her granite palace gushed forth pure perennial streams, which are joined by a thousand mountain springs that constitute the head waters of the picturesque Chattahoochee river, and like the rivers which run out of the garden of Eden, abound in gold.

The cries of the wolf and the night-hawk disturbed not the slumbers of the youthful lovers. But Nacoochee and Sautee could no more hide themselves from the revengeful savages than could Adam and Eve hide from the presence of the father of the human family, after having listened to the beguiling serpent and eaten of the forbidden fruit. A savage shout announced the capture of the foe who had dared to rob the old chief of his daughter. Hasty judgment was pronounced; Sautee was to be thrown, in the presence of Nacoochee, from the highest precipice on Mt. Yonah. Before the sentence was executed, the warriors engaged in a death song and war-dance around the strongly guarded prisoner. This was kept up until the setting sun had dropped behind the western mountains, and the evening star was looking down upon the tragic scene. At a signal from the old chief, four strong warriors seized Sautee, and with one terific yell hurled him headlong into the chasm beneath. Quick as thought, Nacoochee sprang from the strong embrace of her father, and shouting, Sautee! Sautee! threw herself from the overhanging precipice. Their mangled remains were found side by side in the valley. The terrific shock well nigh broke the heart of the aged father. He directed that Nacoochee and Sautee should be buried on the banks of the Chattahoochee, in one grave, and had a mound raised over them to mark the spot. This mound is now the property of Mr. C. L. Williams, eldest son of the late Major Edward Williams. It has been planted in vines and blue grass. The cypress, ivy and rhododendron cover the graves of Nacoochee and Sautee.

The valleys of Nacoochee and Sautee, which are twin sisters and unite just below the residence of Col. E. P. Williams, were named to perpetuate the memory of the young Cherokee girl and her Choctaw lover.

CHAPTER IX.

Clarksville, the county seat of Habersham county, is situated on the Soque river, eight miles above its junction with the Chattahoochee. The picturesque grandeur of the scenery surrounding it; the lofty peaks of the Blue Ridge crowding the horizon, like stern visaged priests, chanting the *vanitas vanitatum* of earthly hopes and joys; the gorgeous sunsets, that hang their curtains of scarlet, blue and purple rare, around these tabernacles of God's power, all seem to whisper to the inhabitants—

> "Muse on God softly, offer a pure heart,
> For meekly thus to serve Him, is thy part."

But the silent teachings of these marvellous works are lost upon the people, if one might take the physiognomy of the village as an indication of the character of its inhabitants; a pretentious exclusiveness being the marked feature of the place.

The shops and smaller houses on the principal streets do not range themselves in regular rows, but each one separates itself from the others by divers palings, yards and fences; and each strives, by some architectural ornament, or by placing itself nearer or farther from the street than its immediate neighbor, to attract the special attention of the passer by; while the larger houses, not satisfied with even this distinction, have sealed themselves on the adjacent hills, and, surrounding themselves with extensive grounds, seem saying to those below—"Stand afar off, for I am more holy than thou." These are the summer residences of wealthy men from South Carolina and lower Georgia, who come up every year with their families, bringing crowds of company, who either stay with their friends, or board at the hotels, and thus give an artificial excitement to the town, though they have very little to do with the people, being quite sufficient to themselves.—The churches, four in number, partake of the disposition of their congregations, and retire in lofty seclusion to the least frequented portion of the town; while the three hotels, though compelled by the nature of their business to seek the public places, seem to do so under protest, and endeavor to look as indifferent about patronage as possible.

Such being the general aspect of the town, our party felt no disposition to linger, and, though it was already late in the evening, they only stopped long enough to procure a guide, and pushed on in the direction of Tallulah Falls, distant twelve miles.

An incident illustrative of of the chivalric spirit of the young men of Clarksville, occurred just as the party was driving off. One of the young ladies dropped her veil, and the wind wafted it within a few paces of a pompous looking young gent in a full suit of white linen, who was sauntering across the square. Without pretending to pick it up, he called out that one of the ladies had dropped a veil, and coolly walked off, leaving the article to be replaced by one of the gentlemen of our party, who descended from one of the carriages for the purpose.

This incident kept them all amused for some time, but, at length fatigue and hunger began to have their effect even on their light hearts, and there were many anxious inquiries of the guide as to the distance to the Falls and a general wish for some haven of rest. This did not present itself for several miles ;no signs of human habitation being seen except a few miserable log huts, breaking now and then the monotony of the pines that lined the road.

The evening grew chilly and more cheerless as night appreached, the heavy atmosphere and wailing wind proving that the storm, which the cloud on Mt. Yonah had foretold, was now close at hand, and the weary travelers began to heartily regret not remaining to test the hospitalities of Clarksville; though Falstaff, who had the guide with him, drove merrily on as if assured of a warm welcome ere long, and the rest were obliged to follow.

Suddenly, just as the patience of the most forbearing began to give way, they emerged from the woods directly in front of a moderate sized frame house, surrounded by a neat yard and numerous outbuildings. Upon the porch sat a large motherly looking old woman dressed in a blue and yellow homespun dress, a check apron, and wide bordered cap, and leisurely smoking a short pipe.

The homelike look of the whole place touched a responsive chord in each heart, and doleful were the faces when Falstaff, who had been to the house, returned with the announcment that they could not stay all night. The necessity was so urgent, that another deputation was dispatched to parley with her, and the good lady at length relented, and agreed to give up one room and the hall to their use, and allow them to occupy a neighboring grove with the horses and carriages. Even these scanty accommodations were eagerly caught at, and they quickly took possession of their new quarters. They found the house scrupulously neat and clean, the snowy beds giving promise of a pleasant night's rest—just then the most desirable thing in the world; but before this could be obtained, the wants of the inner man must be attended to, and the common question:—"What shall we have for supper?" was not very easy of solution when it concerned a meal for twenty-eight in that backwoods country.

The principal objection to entertaining them urged by their hostess had been the ill-behavior of a party who had stopped there the week before, but the polite bearing and quiet manners of *our* party, had already impressed the good lady so favorably that she readily agreed to allow them the use of her neat kitchen, and furnish whatever they might need from her dairy. They were all thoroughly tired of cold bread, and there was a general outcry for a warm supper; so, though there was no stove, a portion of the ladies set themselves to work to cook a meal.

The negro drivers were directed to make a fire in the immense fire-place that occupied one end of the kitchen; Miss Patty filled the tea kettle and hung it over the blaze; Lady Montague made biscuits which Lady Capulet baked in a spider; the sentimental Iola showed herself an adept in dressing and frying chickens. Aunt Quimby made the coffee, while Mrs. Page, with the assistance of the gay colored china from Mrs. Anderson's corner cupboard, set the table in a more civilized fashion than had yet blessed their Bohemian life; and, when the gentlemen were called in to supper, they found a goodly meal of hot biscuits and corn bread, fried chickens and cold ham, butter, milk, and hot coffee, to which they did ample justice, and paid many compliments to the fair cooks.

The meal was scarcely over and everything housed for the night, when the rain descended in torrents. The knowledge that they had a shelter from the fury of the storm, only made the sense of comfort deeper as they gathered around the lightwood fire which had been kindled in the sitting-room of the family, which consisted of Mr. Anderson, his wife, and several grown sons and daughters; but they were all too weary for much fun, and the ladies soon dropped off one by one to their room to find that the matrons had, with Mrs. Anderson's permission, moved the feather beds on the floor, leaving the mattresses on the steads, and thus forming four comfortable beds large enough to contain them all; and in these they soon disposed themselves for dreamless slumbers that lasted uninterrupted till morning. The gentlemen were equally comfortable, if one might judge from the loud snoring that proceeded from the hall where they had made their beds.

CHAPTER X.

When they awoke in the morning the rain had ceased, and though the clouds were still dark and lowering, faint gleams of clear sky, and the merry voices of bird and insect life gave promise of a clear day, which was verified by the sudden appearance of the sun while the party was lingering over their late breakfast.

As it was Sunday, it was decided to make it indeed, a day of rest both to man and beast, by remaining in their present quarters till the evening, and the party scattered each to follow the bent of his own inclination in whiling away the hours. Some took advantage of the leisure to write letters and journalize; some read; others more devout stole off and,

"in the darkling wood.
Amid the cool and silence, knelt down
And offered to the mightiest solemn thanks
And supplication."

On every heart was a Sabbath stillness, a delicious sense of peace and quietude evoked by the panorama of loveliness around them, and only known to those who appreciate the beautiful in nature and art. Ere noon, however, they were to see another aspect of Nature's face, for they were all driven into the house, and for the first time witnessed the majesty of a storm amid these mountain heights. The deep grating of the thunder, as it reverated from peak to peak, the vivid flashes of lightning that leaped in forked chains from cloud to cloud, the deep roaring of the wind, and the rush of many waters among the mountain gorges; all contributed to make up a scene of wild sublimity, that, like all the sterner aspects of the Almighty's power, awed while it delighted.

Thunder storms among the mountains are, however, generally of short duration, and this soon passed off to the lowlands, and the gentlemen went out to feed the horses preparatory to starting. Lady Montague proposed that, as this was the time they were generally at church, they should all join in singing some hymns. The note books were produced, though, through deference to the uncultivated tastes of the family, only familiar tunes were selected; but one of the matrons came in after a few minutes to tell them that Mrs. Anderson said that was not what *she* called singing, she liked the "fa si la style," and the choir gave up indespair.

By 12 o'clock they were again on the way to the Falls, distant five miles. The road lay through a country so wild and uncultivated as to be almost savage. God created both the roaring cataract and the gentle purling stream, both have their office in the economy of nature, but how widely differernt their effect upon their surroundings. The course of a smoothly gliding stream may be easily traced through the landscape by the luxuriant vegetation that seeks its banks. Tall birch, silvery-barked sycamores, and graceful willows and alders bend over the stream, watching the reflections of their own beauties in the pellucid mirror and nodding and coquetting with the dancing ripples; while at their feet the purple violets, modest daisies, blue-fringed gentian, meek-eyed forget-me-nots, feathery ferns, sweet scented heartleaves, and thousands of other plants love to congregate and play at hide and seek among the rich grass which mark the path of the life-giving waters. But these graceful shrubs and plants seem to shrink away affrighted by "the whitening sheet," "silver splendors" and dashing waters which weave the "enamled arras of the rainbow," and the banks of the cataract are generally barren and sterile, or, if vegetation appears it is in the form of the hardy pine, or sturdy oak, those pioneers of the vegetable kingdom, accustomed to, and undaunted by the war of elements. Now it seemed as if in penetrating into the arcana of Nature's mysteries, they were leaving all the footprints of man behind them. The road grew from bad to worse; in many places they were obliged to alight and walk over spots where only the most careful driving could transport the empty vehicles. No sound broke the stillness, save now and then the rush and roar of some mountain stream, tumbling over the rocks in frantic haste, and the melancholy sighing of the wind in the tall pines that shut in the road. Even the voice of insect life seemed to have deserted the neighborhood of the gorge of waters, the thunder of whose voice they were momentarily expecting to hear.

After a time the woods grew more open, and the broken road descending a steep hill, stopped suddenly in front of a crazy looking building, which seemed to bar all further advance in that direction. The guide informed them that the descent from there to the river, distant about half a mile, was so steep as to be unsafe for the carriages, which would have to be left at the house before them, known as Beal's House.

Both building and inmates were of a very unprepossessing appearance, and, after some discussion, it was determined to leave the various articles in the carriages in care of the two servants while the party made a descent to the falls. No time was to be lost, as it was already late in the evening, and each gentleman selecting a partner, hurried off after the guide down the narrow path that led from the back of the house to the river, and soon reached the edge of the gorge, where, hundred of feet below, the imprisoned waters fight and rage against their rocky barriers like things of life.

The Tallulah river is the western branch of the Tugaloo, and here seems to tear its way directly through a range of mountains more than a mile in length, forming an awful gulf, varying in width from three to six hundred feet, and walled in by stupendous fronts of solid rock, impregnable to the assaults of man.

Down these perpendicular walls of rock small streams pour into the river at different points, forming four beautiful cascades, known as Stair-way, Hawthorne, Vandevere, and Ribbon, Cassades. The descent to the bed of the stream can only be made on the west side by the tracts of former rivulets that have worn hollows in the solid rock down which a precarious foothold may be found by the aid of the shrubbery that grows in the hollows.

Not deterred by these difficulties, the younger portion of the party prepared to make the descent. The guide, armed with a long stick, took the lead and the others followed in couples, the gentlemen bearing the children in their arms. For a time the route, though descending constantly, was comparatively smooth, but they soon struck the ravine worn by the water, and then came the tug of war; the path being so narrow and precipitous that it was with difficulty they could keep their feet.

Some crabbed old bachelor has asserted that there are two things that were never intended for locomotion, viz: ducks and women; but he would have changed his mind could he have seen the activity with which the ladies, though encumbered with crinoline, overcame the obstacles in their path; creeping over some, around others, and swinging themselves from point to point by the aid of the bushes with an agility that bade fair to rival their male companions; laughing at each mishap, and enduring fatigue not only with fortitude, but a gayety that produced strange echoes among these frightful solitudes.

About half way down the cliff, they came to a spot which might be very appropriately termed the "jumping-off place," as the path runs over the face of a sheer descent of ten or twelve feet, which can only be passed by swinging down by the bushes to the next ledge, which is so narrow that you are suspended over the foaming maelstorm of waters, hundreds of feet below. Even the most adventuresome of the ladies paused at this obstacle, and it required a good deal of persuasion from the guide to induce them to proceed. At length Aunt Quimby allowed herself to be lifted down by Rashleigh Obaldiston's strong arms, and she was followed by all the young people, except Miss Patty Pace, who decided to remain with the matrons and children, they having declined risking their necks further.

A few yards of careful creeping along the ledge brought them to a place where a huge stone had fallen from the top and lodging against a flat surface of the cliff, formed a narrow passage of several yards in length, only to be passed by crawling on the hands and knees, and known as "Reed's Squeeze" from the fact that a large man of that name had become so tightly fastened in its narrow confines that he could only be extricated with great difficulty.

While the guide explained the origin of its name, there was a general anxiety as to how Falstaff, who weighed largely over two hundred, would accomplish the feat, repeated calls to him not to attempt it until all the company reached the spot. He very good-naturedly waited till all came up, and then went through safely, but with so many queer remarks and grimaces, that the rocks rung with their shouts of merriment.

A few steps further and a scene of such wondrous sublimity burst upon their view that both words and laughter were checked and they stood—

> "Amazed—confounded— blinded with the blaze
> Of concentrated beauty."

They had now reached the bed of the river, which is here chafed and maddened by its angry rush of several thousand feet over the Rapids above the Falls.

Suddenly, as if gathering up its full power for the leap, it whirls rapidly around the face of a prjoecting cliff, and flings itself headlong over the cataract of Tempesta, filling the gorge with its tumultuous roaring, and scattering clouds of spray over the hardy evergreens that cling to every crevice of the belting cliffs overhead. The height ot the ledge is 140 feet, horizontal shoot of the water 14½ feet, depth of chasm at this point 245 feet, width 350.

A better idea of height and depth can rarely be attained than that presented by the fall of Tempesta. One feels there as if he had penetrated to the very center of the earth. In the half twilight which fills this chasm, where none but the noontide rays ever penetrate, every thing is seen in dim and misty hues, and no sound is heard but the wild dashing of the turbulent waters, and the weird voices of the wind, sounding like the shrieks of lost spirits condemned for eternity to these dark recesses; while overhead bends a sky as pure and bright as the heaven from which they have been banished.

The wish of each heart, when the first feeling of awe struck admiration had passed, was that they could imprint the scene before them upon some more tangible tablet than that of memory, and in this they were gratified by a chance encounter with a party of artists, who were taking stereoscopic views of the various Falls; and to their skill, these sketches are indebted for the illustrations which we have been unable to have inserted in this edition.

As it was growing late in the evening, the guide hurried them to reascend, so as to obtain a view from another point before night. If the *descent* had been difficult, the *ascent* was still more so. Cap declared that she never realized how much lean people had to be thankful for, till she saw the strenuous exertions, and spinal contortions of Lady Montague, Falstaff, and Mrs. Gummidge, the fat ones of the party.

Once at the top they paused at a spring to quaff what, indeed, seemed to be "waters of life" to their thirsty spirits, but which were very near causing an accident that would have changed all their mirth to mourning. The spring was much nearer the edge of the cliff than any ot them supposed, as it was surrounded by a dense growth of bushes, and the Historian in a playful race with Cap to gain possession of the dipper, ran too near the edge, and only saved himself from falling over the dizzy height by clutching at a neighboring limb, which was fortunately strong enough to sustain his weight till he could regain his footing.

"You and I were very near taking an unintentional leap, just then ; I wonder if they would have named the spot "Lover's Leap," he said to Cap, trying to laugh at the terror which had driven the color from every cheek ; but his tremulous voice told that he realized the danger he had escaped, and he hurried them away from the dangerous locality.

Another short and comparatively smooth descent brought them to the "Devil's Pulpit." This is a solid mass of grey freestone, like an old fashioned pulpit. The hollow booming of the waters at its base, the clouds of spray that fill the a r, the awful chasm with its boiling, seething and raging waters which it overlooks, all suggest the horrors of the bottomless pit, and, probably won for it its name. The top is flat, almost circular in form, and affords a pleasant resting place except when the sun is directly overhead, whon its rays are reflected with such power from the white surface of the sandstone as to dazzle the eyes and blister the feet.

From the top is a splendid view of Oceanna.

The perpendicular height of this fall is 92 feet, horizontal pitch of the water 20 1-2 feet. The river at this point seems to have reached the heart of the mountains, the depth of the chasm being 413 feet, width 600 feet. Words fail to give an idea of the silver splenders of this fall, framed in its dark back-ground of rocks and trees, and our party would fain have lingered for hours gazing upon its beauties, had not the waning light warned them that no time was to be lost in seeking shelter for the night ; and they turned reluctantly away, promising themselves to return on the morrow when the presence of the sun would add additional charms.

CHAPTER XI.

They reached the place where they had left the carriages to find that the servants had transferred their contents to the house, which looked even more gloomy in the grey twilight than when viewed by daylight. It was a two-story building in almost the last stage of dilapidation; the broken roof having fallen in in several places, and one end of the half-tumbled down piazza being used as a wagon shed. The inmates, consisting of an old woman and several young ones, were as unprepossessing as their house; but, as it was the only available shelter within five miles, the gentlemen proceeded to make the best arrangements they could for the night. They were only able to engage one room, the others being occupied by the artists. This was found to be as dirty and uncomfortable as could well be imagined, but the ladies, wet, tired and hungry as they were, set themselves to make the best of their surroundings by having a large lightwood fire kindled, and sweeping the floor throughly. Then, while some rested and dried their damp clothes, others brought wood and water and made preparations for supper. Fortunately nothing was to be done but make a pot of strong coffee; and, while this was boiling, they were called out in the yard to see the Hermit, who had accompained the artists' party from the fall. It was so dark that they could only distinguish a tall figure dressed in white clothes to whom the gentleman were talking in loud tones, as if he were deaf, but gaining very little beyond monosyllabic replies, uttered in a strange monotonous sounding voice. He invited the party to visit him the next day, but positively declined their urgent invitation to remain and take supper with them, though he accepted some ears of green corn which they had just purchased, and with these under his arm, bowed low to them all, and took the direction of his lonely hut.

Supper being ready, the ladies insisted that their companions in misery—the artists—should be invited to join them. The invitation was accepted. They proved to be well known gentlemen of Athens, and, though most of the viands were cold and served in tin plates and cups, the meal was a merrier one than is often eaten from cut-glass and silver. The conversation ran upon the Hermit and his eccentricities, about which the ladies were very curious, and the artists narrated various incidents of his life there which made them more anxious than ever to see him in his hermitage.

He had arrived amid these solitudes during the winter of 1866, but, as the Falls are never visited at that season, his presence was not discovered until the ensuing spring. He had built him a rude cabin of logs in the vicinity of the Falls, and had remained there for the past two years, holding little communication with any one except Esquire Vandevere, an aged hunter and trapper of the Tallulah Mountains, who was a celebrated Indian fighter in the days when the red skins held Northeastern Georgia, and is the counterpart of Cooper's hero of the forest—Natty Bumpo—the Leather Stocking.

The Hermit gave his name as John Cole, but refused to tell whence he came, or the object of his sojourn in these dreary solitudes.

When supper was over, the younger portion of the company dispersed in various directions; some to sit in the carriages till bedtime, other sentimental pairs to promenade the piazza, oblivious of the inequalities in the floor.

It was late when the parties separated, the artists invitimg the gentlemen to share their room, and the ladies retiring to theirs, but not to sleep.

The bed, the single article of furniture the room contained, had been, upon inspection, pronounced entirely untenable, and they had decided to pass the night upon the floor; but Manolia, who had visited the Falls the year before, and stayed in the same room, gave so thrilling an account of the horrors she had endured from the bed-bugs and other vermin with which the house was infested, that it drove sleep effectually from their eyes. Besides, every attempt they made to dispose themselves in the space allotted them by the matrons, only demonstrated the truth of the philosophical maxim that two bodies cannot occupy the same space at the same time, till Aunt Quimby declared that they reminded her of children's toy blocks, which, if properly fitted together, the box in which they were bought, will exactly contain them, but try any other way, and the last one will displace all the rest. As there appeared to be no master builder among them, she proposed they should stop trying to fit themselves together, and have all the fun they could till morning.

This proposition was received with such enthusiasm that it awoke Lady Montague, who, worried at being aroused from her first nap, proceeded to administer a severe reprimand to Manolia, who was her niece, meanwhile hitting the whole party some clever licks over her shoulders. Manolia, who was a tender hearted little thing, shed a few quiet tears in the corner of the blanket allotted to her, but the others only laughed, while gentle Mrs. Page was roused to their defence, and declared the girls were excusable for making a noise when it was impossible for them to sleep. Thus encouraged, the fun waxed fast and furious, Miss Patty Pace contributing no small amount by her queer antics. That good lady and Mrs. Gummidge declaring that they intended to make a better impression on the Hermit than the others, fell to work washing various articles of clothing which they hung on chairs around the fire to dry; and it required such vigorous exertions on the part of Miss Patty to prevent their being overthrown by the restless movements of the others, that she at length declared she believed she was snake-bit, and must take some of the medicine provided for such occasions; and diving into the trunk, produced the black bottle and proceeded to test its contents. But in vain she shook and tasted; nothing but honey would come, and her queer speeches and grimaces kept them all in convulsions of laughter, though they did not discover till the next morning that she had gotten the wrong bottle, and was drinking strained honey all the time.

Mrs. Gummidge had appropriated two chairs and a trunk for her sleeping place, and permitted Aunt Quimby to sit in a chair and make a pillow of her body; and the last sound the writer heard that night was Lady Capulet requesting some one to put their feet on her, for she was like the little Irish boy whose mother was covering him with a door, "It was not everybody that had feet to cover with."

So passed the first day and night at Tallulah.

CHAPTER XII.

The night passed so uncomfortably that most of the girls were glad to rise at day-light under the excuse of fufilling an engagement made the night before to see the sun rise over the Ocean View.

This is a high point about a mile from the Falls where the eye can wander for miles over a level country, and as in the dim twilight of early morning, you cannot see the range of low mountains that bound it in the far distance, you seem, indeed gazing upon the "blue illimitable sea;" and the illusion is farther heightened by the mists rising from the numerous streams threading the country, that look like foam-capped billows rolling shoreward, while the distant roar of the Falls seems

> "But the noise of WAVES
> Dashing against the shore,
> And the wind from some bleaker quarter
> Mingling with its roar."

Over this scene, when the party reached the spot, still hung the dim hues of night, and all nature seemed waiting with hushed breath the advent of the sun, whose rosy heralds were transforming the east into a scene of glory, and tinting the vapors below with the most delicate tinge of red. Another moment, and the voice of God seemed to re-echo over those mountain summits, uttering tnat sublime fiat, "Let there be Light"—and there was light, as the sun shot above the horizon.

* * * * * * *

> "I've been roaming, I've been roaming
> Where the MOUNTAIN dews is sweet,
> And I am coming, I am coming;
> With its pearls upon my feet—"

sang Meg half an hour afterwards, dancing gaily into the dilapidated kitchen where the elders, with rather grum looks, the effects of last night's discomfort, were making preparations for breakfast. "Good people, if you had gone with us you could have taken such draughts from Nature's fountain as would have made you forget such sublunary things as eating and drinking.

"I think I should prefer a draught of something more tangible this morning," said Mrs. Gummidge, sourly. "And you will make a pretty appearance before strangers with your draggled dress."

"Well, that will only give you and Miss Patty a better chance to make an impression in your clean clothes," she answered laughingly; and, the balance of the walking party having now entered, their gay spirits soon routed the azure imps, and all proceded with fresh energy to their domestic tasks. Aunt Quimby, declaring that she was growing gramnivarious from long abstinence from vegetable food, went out in the neglected garden to search for salads, but could only find some tomatoes, which she proceeded to prepare by a Virginia receipt. Cap, Meg and Mrs. Gummidge prepared a large oven of stewed corn, regretting the absence of beans to form a succotash. Ladies Montague and Capulet made biscuit in the same tray in the most amicable manner, and the rest bustled around setting the table in the yard, declaring it sacrilege to exchange the bright sunshine for such a house. The gentlemen rendered what aid they could, and to such a height did their merriment rise, that it was only after four trials that the artist succeeded in keeping them still long enough to take a photograph of the breakfast party.

The meal being at length dispatched, hasty preparations were made for another descent, and it was amusing to a looker-on to watch the sly manouvers among both ladies and gentlemen to secure as companions those they liked most; for though it had been proclaimed that there was not a Romeo and Juliet in the party, there were several couples that, divide them as you would, were sure to be near each other again in a few minutes; and there was, probably, the usual amount of jealousy and heart burnings, for, noble as were the natures of those composing the party, in temper, which Lever calls "the great coats of humanity," there was the diversity usual among such a crowd.

It had been decided that they should first visit the Hermit in his retreat. A narrow path, winding for some distance through the thickest of the woods that covered the plateau above the Falls, led to the Hermitage. It was a low cabin built of rough logs, fitted together with no better instrument than an ax and covered with rough clap-boards. At one end was a stone chimney, while the space before the door was surrounded by pine poles supported on posts, and some attempt at ornamentation made by clearing away the underbrush and laying the ground off in the shape of a star.

Their knock at the low door was answered by the guide whom they had not seen before that morning; and in a few minutes the Hermit made his appearance. He was a young man of about twenty-four, of medium height, florid complexion, dark brown eyes, moustache and hair; the latter, worn in long elf-locks on his shoulders. The whole appearance of the man denoted one fond of the good things and social pleasures of life, but this convivial disposition was poorly concealed under a mask of studied gravity and humility. He never lifted his eyes to the circle of blooming faces around him, but invited them to enter his humble dwelling in an affected drawl with his eyes upon the ground.

Falstaff, the spokesman of the party, declined the invitation, as they were anxious to make as many descents as possible. The recluse regretted not being able to accompany them as he had promised to guide the artists to some points inaccessible to ladies but hoped to see them again during the day, and that they would call as they came back.

"He need not have put that 'again' in that last polite

speech of his," said Meg, as the party moved on, "for he has not seen us the first time yet, unless it be the hems of our robes. Mrs. Gummidge must have had a hint of his peculiarities when she washed the mud out of hers last night."

"Perhaps he goes on the principle that, 'all's well that ends well,'" said Lady Capulet. "If so, he has formed a deplorable opinion of most of us."

"It is my opinion that the Hermit is a humbug," said Cap, sententiously.

"Why; because he did not look at any of you?" asked the Historian, who heard the last remark.

"No, Sir; but because his appearance, manner and mode of life are affected in the extreme. His face bears no likeness to those

> "Holy men who hide themselves
> Deep in the woody wilderness, and give
> Their lives to thought and prayer."

On the contrary, it brought before my mind, Friar Tuck, and I will wager anything, that, like that jolly Hermit, he keeps 'dried peas and other pulse,' for the entertainment of his guests, and regales himself in private on venison patties."

"Or on sardines," said Mrs. Gummidge, "for I saw a number of boxes thrown out round his house, and Roscius says he threw away the corn we gave him last night before he had gone five yards from the house."

"The guide tells me he gave him an excellent breakfast of fried chicken, eggs, and other nice things," said Falstaff. "I almost wish I had accepted his invitation to eat with him."

"I expect he is some escaped convict hiding from the officers of the law," said the Historian, but this suggestion received but small favor from some of the ladies of the party, who had been captivated by his handsome face, and the air of mystery which surrounded him.

Thus conversing they reached the head of the ravine down which their course lay. It was even rougher than the descent of the evening before, and required the most careful footing, so that conversation was impossible, beyond a call for help now and then, as some of the ladies became entangled in the roots and bushes that beset their way. So rapid was the inclination, that in spite of Falstaff's gasped injunctions "to go slow," the whole party were in a run most of the time. A few yards from the bottom, Lord Chesterfield and Mrs. Gummidge, who happened to be together, both lost their footing, went sliding down the cliff, and, not stopping at the bottom, went feet foremost into a cavern in the rock, leaving their heads and shoulders outside. Fortunately, no bones were broken by their tumble, and the only injuries being a few bruises and blushes, the affair was forgotton in a hearty laugh, and they gave their attention to the scenery.

They were now upon the verge of Hawthorn's Pool.

This pool, situated between the falls of Oceanna and Hurricane, was the scene of a terrible accident nineteen years before. A young tourist of the name of Hawthorne, was precipitated by accident, into the pool, and, instantly disappearing from sight, was never seen again in life. His mangled body was afterwards found at the foot of Hurricane Fall. The water wears a look of the greatest placidity, mirroring in its bosom the overhanging rocks and trees, but it has probably a rapid rotary current at the bottom, as any object thrown in instantly disappears from view. Looking up the river from the tree that almost bridges the pool, the most striking object is a distant view of the Devil's Pulpit.

The skill of the artist produced as good a picture of this as the distance and surrounding foliage would allow, and, viewed with a telescope, the peculiar characteristic of this structure, built without hands, can be clearly traced; and in its silent majesty and grandeur speaks of him "who marked for the sun his journey, and bade the moon know her going down." far more forcibly than the voice of the most eloquent preacher.

As the morning was wearing away rapidly, they could not stay very long at one point, and retracing their steps for a short distance struck into the path that leads to the banks of L'Ean d' Or. The feature that most strikes the attention of the tourist in approaching this cataract, is the perpendicular wall of rock that towers above him for two hundred feet, and which is worn by the action of the water into grotesque figures. The party amused themselves by tracing a likeness to familiar things in these fissures. One saw a goat, another an arm chair, another a profile; while the more romantic caught glimpses of mossy towers, rock bound castles, impregnable fortresses and overhanging battlements, which might have been the abodes of the Titans when they played at football with the hills and mountains.

Approaching nearer to the river bank the full splendors of the cataract burst upon their view. The perpendicular height of L'Ean D'Or is only 32 feet; from the base to the top 70 feet. The descent being less rapid, the water comes down with a more even flow than at the other cataracts, and the unbroken sheet, reflecting from its bosom the full rays of the noonday sun, has obtained for it its name of "Water of Gold." Near the centre of the fall is a projecting stone, the end of which is worn into a fantastic likeness to an animals face, and it looks like some huge sea monster looking out over the turbid waters.

Two falls remained to be seen, but through the incompetency of the guide, they were not visited by any of our party. Capitola, alone, by a succession of daring ventures, which nearly threw the other ladies of the party into convulsions, and seriously alarmed the gentlemen, managing to catch a glimpse of them from a distance. The artist, however, made several visits to them, and succeeded in obtaining a good stereoscopic view of Hurricane Falls.

The Hermit, who with the assistance of Esquire Vandevere had taken the measurements of all the prominent places about the Falls, furnished the following dimensions: Perpendicular height 52 feet from the base to the top 110 feet. Depth of chasm at this point, 495 feet, width, 550 feet. There is another small fall six hundred feet below Hurricane, called Serpentine, but so difficult of access that it is very seldom visited, and no position can be found from which a sterescopic view can be obtained. The perpendicular height is 23 feet, from the base to the top 80 feet.

The river, having now done its work of tearing asunder the mountains, rapidly loses its tempestuous character, though the impetus given the water by its successive plunges is seen in its arrowy rush over the rapids below the falls. Looking down from the foot of Ribbon Cascade you can see the banks gradually widening and lowering to the ordinary height above common water mark, while the stream, making a sudden bend to the west, leaves the mountains behind it and flows on through fertile lowlands to its junction with the Chattooga ten miles below.

The guide representing the other falls to be inaccessible, the party reluctantly retraced their steps to the Hermitage, to find a note tacked on the door apologizing for the absence, of its master and requesting the ladies to enter and rest themselves. They accepted the invitation, but found little to gratify their curiosity. A cot bedstead, a corner cupboard, one chair, and a few books comprised the entire furniture. There was a small kiln in the yard which he was said to use for cooking purposes, though no eatables of any kind were to be seen. The resources of the house were soon exhausted, and after writing their names upon the paper which seemed to have been placed for the purpose, they returned towards the house, pausing to catch one other view of Tempesta from the Devil's Pulpit.

Seating themselves in comfortable positions there they listened while Miss Quimby read aloud the following story.

CHAPTER XIII.

THE LEGEND OF TALLULAH.

On the beautiful banks of the Tallulah river stood a simple, but neat, dwelling. Though the walls were of rough hewn logs, the climbing vines over the doors and windows redeemed their harshness, while the furniture within wore an air of cleanliness that told of refined tastes among these dwellers of the wilderness. John Goodwin's own sturdy right arm had redeemed this spot from the forest around, and hither he had brought his wife and infant babes to share with him the hardships and toils, as well as the pure waters and life giving airs of this mountain home. His wife, Esther, a woman of uncommon energy of character, had uncomplainingly given up home and friends to follow her husband beyond the remotest bounds of civilization; and here, cut off from all society, the true strength and purity of woman's love displayed itself in brightening and adorning by her industry and skill their forest home, and making herself, indeed, the light of her husband's eyes; seeking no other companionship during his daily absences in the fields than the wonders of nature spread out around her. The lofty grandeur of the mountains, the solemn stillness of the forest, unbroken save by the ceaseless thunder of Tallulah Falls, only a short distance from her dwelling, filled her mind with lofty images and beautiful thoughts, which she never dreamed of expressing even to her husband, whose plain sturdy sense was apt to laugh at these fanciful thoughts and romantic dreams of his wife.

There were none but friendly Indians around them, for the Cherokees were at peace with the white men, and the tribe having become accustomed to their presence among them, paid them many little acts of kind attention, which they returned by assisting them in many of the arts of which they were ignorant; and among these simple hearted people, the "Great Medicine Man," as they termed Goodwin, was a person of great importance to be consulted in every emergency of their uneventful life.

Thus years wore on till marks of advancing age were to be

seen on the brows of both Goodwin and his wife, and their two sons had grown into stout boys of twelve and fourteen, who assisted their father in cultivating the fields, which now extended for acres around their dwelling; while their daughter, now sixteen, bloomed fair as the wild rose from which she took her English name, though she was known among the Indians as Swannoa, meaning the *Beautiful*. As her daughter grew up to womanhood the mother's heart inclined more constantly towards the home in North Carolina where her own happy girlhood had been passed, and she said every year, "I will persuade her father to send Rose back to our own people to be educated;" but the year passed, and the mother's heart still refused to part with her darling.

At length there came a winter whose severity had not been equalled in the memory of the oldest inhabitant; and, in that mountainous region, all creatures exposed to its influence suffered severely. The Indians, improvident by nature and habit, considering only the wants of the day, were soonest liable to any influence that effected the means of subsistence which the fields and forests yielded, and cases of suffering were soon very common among them. These, whenever known, were promptly relieved by Goodwin and his wife, but their small stores could do but little for the hundreds around them whose privations soon brought on an epidemic fever which swept them off by hundreds.

A slow and lingering spring at length began to dawn on the land, though winter, the stern old warrior, still lingered upon the mountain tops, ready to take advantage of any incautious movement of the forces mustering in the valleys, and fast showing their strength in the crimson banners of the maple, and the upspringing spears upon the hillsides. Goodwin was once more busily at work in the fields, but his wife noticed that there was a gloom upon his brow, while the trusty rifle, which had rarely been removed from its post of honor over the fireplace save on the occasion of some deer or turkey hunt, was now his constant companion; and she soon learned the cause of his anxiety from the squaws who were daily visitors. They said that many miles away towards the rising sun, there lived a tribe, the bitter enemies of the Cherokees. These, learning of the suffering of the tribe in the Tallulah mountains, were preparing to make an invasion upon them, in which case, both Whites and Indians were likely to suffer alike, and that her husband had been warned of their common danger by the warriors of their tribe, who were on the alert to repel the threatened invasion of the Choctaws.

But the mild bright days crept by without any fresh incentive to their fears, and the awakening beauties of the spring began to banish all apprehension from their minds, and life settled back into its accustomed quiet channels.

One morning Goodwin and his sons went to a distant field to work, saying that they might not return at the usual dinner hour, as they were anxious to finish planting a piece of corn. Goodwin carried his gun as usual, though he said to his wife on leaving that his only use of it would probably be to shoot the wild pigeons which were flying over in large flocks; and, chucking his daughter under the chin, bade her prepare herself to make a famous pigeon pie on his return.

The hours of the morning passed swiftly both to Rose and her mother, each busy about domestic duties. More than once in passing out of doors, Rose thought she detected moving forms on the edge of the woods nearest the house, but they gave her no uneasiness, for the Indians were generally abroad at this season in search of the berries which formed a large portion of their subsistence.

As the sun touched the noon mark, the horn used for the purpose was sounded to summon the laborors to their dinner, but they did not come; and, after waiting a short time, Rose proposed to her mother that she should take it to them and bring back the pigeons they might have killed to prepare them for supper. Mrs. Goodwin readily agreed; the bucket was soon prepared, and with a song on her lips the blithe maiden tripped away; her mother's eyes following with pride the lithe form and graceful movements till they were lost in the woods which screened the Falls from view. With fearless step she trod the brink of the awful chasm along which the narrow path wound, undismayed by the foaming waters beneath, and was soon with her father and brothers.

The sun descended towards the west and finally set in flames of crimson and gold, but still she did not return, and, at length her mother went to meet them. She had almost reached the field where she expected to find them, when she was startled by the sound of shots, and a moment after the woods resounded with the terrific warwhoop of the Indian, which the mountain echoes repeated again and again. Breathless with terror, she crept under shelter of some undergrowth, and threw herself flat upon the earth.

A few moments of death-like stillness succeeded the terrible outburst of sound which seemed to have shocked all Nature into quiet, and she tried to collect her thoughts and consider what was best to be done. In a few moments, though no farther sound was heard, her quick eye detected throug the gathering twilight dusky forms flitting from tree to tre and she knew that she was surrounded by hostile Indians. Prostrate she lay, her pale lips forming inarticulate prayers for the safety of her loved ones to that God of her youth whom she had almost forgotten in her wilderness life. Fortunately for her, the Red Skins were too intent upon their object to notice her; onward they crept, stealthily as panthers, and soon another yell rent the silence, and the fiery glare that filled the valley, told that her home was in flames.

How the long hours of that night passed to that lone watcher, none may know but that Eye that never slumbers or sleeps; but, when morning dawned, the wild eyes and blanched hair of the woman that crept from under the bushes told their own tale of fearful agony. She reached the edge of the clearing and looked out. The still smoking ruins of her home met her eyes, but no traces of the Indians were to be seen. At length she summoned up resolution to approach the spot; everything was destroyed save one small outhouse which had probably escaped their sight. No traces of blood, however, were to be seen, and with swift steps she retraced her way. Reaching the field where her husband had been at work, a fearful sight met her eyes. Both of her sons lay dead in the furrow where they had fallen, and a short distance off was their father with his daughter clasped by one arm, and grasping his musket convulsively in the other hand. Each head showed the feartul circle where the scalp lock had been torn away, and life was quite extinct in all.

When the wretched woman realized this, one wild, piercing shriek rent the air, and she fell lifeless upon the dead bodies.

* * * * * * *

Fifteen years had passed, and the stormy wind of a wild December night raved through the forest, and mingled its voice with the thunders of Tallulah Falls, unchanged by the years which had passed since the Creator spoke them into being. Around a hut, standing near the site of the Goodwin dwelling, the wind whistled with such unrestrained fury that it sent the smoke in clouds into the room; but little did the crone crouching closely over the fire heed its whistling save as an unusually loud blast threatened to overturn her frail dwelling, she raised her head, an expression of wild joy passed over her haggard face, and she whispered to herself, "They are coming—the hour of revenge draws near."

As if in answer to her words, a knock was heard at the door of the hut. The hag took a blazing brand from the fire, and, holding it high above her head, opened the door. Without stood an Indian, the towering feathers of whose head-dress as well as his painted face, marked him as a chieftain on the war-path. In a few words of tolerable English he told her that they needed a guide over the windings of Tallulah. The crone objected, though with the same lurking smile on her face. He spoke again in a tone of authority, pointing to the band of warriors behind him, as if determined to enforce his request, and with one glance behind she stepped forth into the storm, and took her way towards the Falls. The Indians followed her in single file without noise of any kind, for they wished to surprise the village which they supposed themselves approaching.

The thunder of the Falls grew louder and louder till it seemed to shock the ear. They reached the Devil's Pulpit; the darkness was intense, and with only one moment's pause to see that the Indians were close behind her, she stepped noiselessly aside. The chieftain passed her and took the fearful step off the edge—it was too dark for the next in the line to miss his form, and he too followed;—one by one they passed into the frightful chasm whose depth gave forth no sound, and as the last one disappeared, the hag threw up her hands with a shriek of fiendish laughter, and exclaiming—"It is finished—I have my revenge," sprung over the fearful ledge and followed her victims. The murder of her husband and children was fearfully avenged.

* * * * * * *

When this story was finished the gentlemen reminded the ladies that it was nearly 3 o'clock in the evening, and, as they had consumed all the provisions brought with them, they had best be making a move, their nearest base of supplies, both for man and beast, being at Mrs. Anderson's, distant five miles; so, with many a last, long, lingering look backward cast at the beauties which had so bewitched them, they took up the line of march for Beal's House. Just before reaching it, they met some tourists who had ridden out from Clarksville to explore the Falls, and a greater contrast than the two parties presented could scarcely be imagined. The one; wet, dirty, weary, torn and ragged from their encounter with bushes, rocks and water; the other; fresh, clean, dainty, and even *distingui* in toilet and appearance. No wonder our party shrunk to one side, and did not realize the force of the old song that in spite of dress,, "A man's a man for 'a that," and they did not regain their self-respect till they gained the carriages. Once within their friendly shelter, the single looking glass was taken from its hiding place and eagerly passed from hand to hand. The images therein reflected could not have been very consoling to their wounded vanity from the grave faces most of them wore for some time. Die, alone, was free from these disquietudes, the evident devotion which spoke from Rashleigh Obaldestone's eyes during their ride in Falstaff's buggy, compensating her for all annoyances, while their evident obliviousness to their surroundings afforded a subject for continual teasing to their companions whenever they came within hailing distance of the ambulance, which they avoided doing as much as possible.

Mrs. Anderson's hospitable house was greeted by the whole party as a temporary home, and the ladies were soon ensconced in their room, from which they emerged about sunset, reinstated in dress and self-esteem. Their hostess, who was expecting their return, had prepared a bountiful supper for them, to which they one and all did ample justice, after which they dispersed to employ the evening according to individual taste. The matrons gathered around the pine-knot fire in the sitting room, which the chill air made pleasant, to enjoy the sensible conversation of their entertainers; the musical portion assembled on the porch and made the echoes ring with their favorite songs, while several sentimental couples promenaded the moon lit yard in blissful forgetfulness of everything but themselves; and it was late before these various parties were willing to relinquish their enjoyments for the sound slumbers which by twelve o'clock reigned undisturbed over the old homestead.

CHAPTER XIV.

"Make haste and pack up the traps girls, while we get the horses. We have no time to loose if we want to see Tacoa to-day," was Falstaff's injunction as he rose from the table the next morning. Obedient to his command, hurry was the order of the day, both in words and deeds, if one might judge from the nimble tongues that kept time to the busy fingers. By the time the horses were harnessed, trunks, baskets and carpet-bags were ready to be stored away in the various vehicles and the ladies once more in traveling garb awaited on the porch their escorts' pleasure, only giving in sly whispers their preference for any particular vehicle or partner.

"I wonder who is going to drive the carriage this morning?" said Die Vernon, with a sly glance in the direction of Rashleigh Obaldistone who stood near her. "*I* am going in it, and I do hope there will be a careful driver, for I hear the road is dreadful."

"Speak a little louder and he will take the hint, Die," said Cap's merry voice at her elbow, her quick eye having detected her friend's *penchant* in that quarter.

Die whirled round on her tormentor with a spirit that showed her name was no misnomer. "I suppose you judge me by yourself, Miss. I have always noticed that those most guilty of artifices themselves soonest suspect them in others."

"On the principle of its being safest to 'set a thief to catch a thief, my dear," retorted Cap, with scarcely a glance at her friend's irate face, as she ran down the steps after Don Quixote, who was on his way to the ambulance with an armful of shawls and blankets. "Don," she called, finding she could not overtake him, "let me ride in front with you?"

"Certainly;" he replied, pausing to make as gallant a bow as his burden would permit, "I shall esteem myself highly honored by such 'goodlie companie'."

They were soon all stored away; Aunt Quimby and Falstaff lead the way, in his buggy, and the incorrigible Cap, seated in the driver's seat of the ambulance, flourished her whip and shouted "Hi Ike and Bill," a command which made Die, who was still angry, arch her brows and elevate her already *retrousse* nose, but which the horses obeyed by putting themselves into a jog trot; and, amid farewells to their hostess, shouts, laughter, and the rumbling of vehicles, the party were on the way to Tocoa.

The road again wound through a dense forest, and once within its gloomy shades the spirits of the party subsided to a mood as sober as their pace, each seemed occupied with their own thoughts, though more than one anxious glance was turned upon the haze that obscured the sun, which, however conducive to reverie, was also probably ominous of a rainy day.

Their forebodings were soon verified by a quick coming shower, which brought Falstaff to a halt so that he might put Aunt Quimby under shelter. The gallant Julius gave her his seat in the ambulance, and prepared to brave the storm in the open buggy, but they had scarcely resumed the line of march, when the breakage of a wheel threw him out on the ground. It was soon ascertained that he was unhurt, but so barren had the trip been of romantic incidents that Miss Patty exclaimed—

"Julius, why in the world did'nt you *pretend* you were stunned, so that Iola might have flown to your assistance, bathed your brow, fanned you with her sighs, and so gotten up an effective tableau?"

"I will remember your suggestions the next time such an accident happens to me, Miss Patty. I was only too glad this time to find I had landed in a soft place, i. e. a dust bank," he said, brushing the dust from his clothes, and pretending not to see Iola's blushes.

The rain had proved only a summer shower, but under the present discouraging aspect of affairs the elders of the party advocated giving up the trip to Tocoa, and turning their faces homeward.

This was promptly vetoed by the younger members; and after much consultation, it was decided that Falstaff should fasten his buggy to the back of the baggage-wagon, and Roscius having volunteered to assist him, they should make their way to Clarksville, distant about ten miles, where they could have the damage repaired, and await their companions.

Lingering adieus were exchanged, for the party did not fancy losing any of its members even for a few hours, especially such an important personage as Falstaff; but nothing better could be done, and with many a lingering look in the direction in which Falstaff and Roscius were already disappearing, the line of march was once more resumed.

The road soon grew so bad that it became evident that the vehicles would have to be relieved of their loads, and the younger ladies of the party decided to accompany the gentlemen on foot. Rashleigh Obaldistone and Capitola lead the way talking in their usual gay strain, seeing which, Die decided to remain in the ambulance with Aunt Quimby, who was taking care of Miss Patty, whose morning gayety was ending with a sick headache.

Don Quixote's sympathy with her sufferings made him drive so slowly over the rough road that the walking party were soon out of sight, though the high hills over which they were traveling bore back an occasional echo of their gay voices. An hour's brisk walking brought the pedestrians to a point where all semblance of a practicable road ended, and they sat down to await the arrival of the carriages, and arrange the flowers which they had gathered.

"Oh, girls," exclaimed Cap, as soon as they were seated, "did you all see that cabin we passed? Now don't you know that any woman must be brave, and love sure enough, to be willing to leave the world, i. e. society, and bring herself in these solitudes in a cabin scarcely large enough to turn round in?"

"How do you know that she has ever known any better?" asked the practical Mrs. Gummidge.

"Why, did'nt you see that beautiful rose which was trained up by the door; an evidence of refinement and cultivation within itself? Rashleigh climbed the fence to get *me* a rose he pretended, but I see he has given Meg the prettiest, and she is ready to sigh—

> "Oh! for a lodge in some vast wilderness,
> Some boundless contiguity of shade."

The inhabitants of that cabin certainly have the last in perfection, but—ugh!—the sighing of the wind in the pines would *ennui* me to death, even if I could stand the other discomforts.

"Miss Cap, when I build a three-story brick, I will ask you to live in it," said the Historian.

"Now you are talking sense, for of course, the more a woman marries, the more she has to love," responded Cap. "But I have too vivid a remembrance of Mrs. J—'s warning that we were to lay no traps for you on this trip, to trust to your promises. *I*, for one, do not lay toils for another's *game dear*."

"I should think not when you wear such a bonnet as that," he retorted pointing to the sun-bonnet with which she was vigorously fanning herself. "Coming up through the woods just now I could have sworn we were following a North Carolina wagon with a cover and when I am near it it requires a telescope to find you in it. What is your fancy for wearing it?"

"My conduct, sir, as you will yet find out, is always based on sound principles," she replied with pretended gravity. "My bonnet is cut on the principle of 'distance lending enchantment,' but if you do not like it, instead of giving me a *three-story brick*, you may send me a white velvet *chapeau* as a bridal present whenever I conclude to make Mr. Nameless the happiest of men. Is not that a fair compromise, Lord Chesterfied?"

"*I* think he would prefer one that bound you to let him furnish your bonnets, and such like traps for the balance of your life, he replied teasingly.

Cap pretended not to notice the significance of his tone, as she darted off to the ambulance which just then drove up to enquire after Miss Patty's health.

She was better, and as it was impossible to proceed any farther with the vehicles, all made preparations to walk the half mile which still lay between them and Tocoa.

If the scenery surrounding Tallulah prepares the mind by its desolate and gloomy features for the rude grandeur denoted by its Indian signification of—*The Terrible*, that around Tocoa harmonizes equally well with the idea of the *Beautiful* so well described by its meaning in the soft Cherokee tongue. The descent of a very steep hill brought the party to a valley or basin about half a mile wide surrounded on every side by hills so lofty as to merit the name of mountains, and which left nothing in common with the outer world visible, save God's own heaven that seemed as near as blue, so lovingly did it bend over the amphitheatre of hills. This sequestered vale was overgrown by a vegetation so luxuriant as to indicate the presence of water even before you caught the murmur of the stream that rippled past to the busy world through an opening between the hills at the entrance of the valley. Silver leaved birches, and sycamores, the giant live-oak, graceful willows, sturdy sweet gums, and other well known forest trees were knit together by flowering vines and creepers forming a wall of living green, that, but for its want of gorgeous coloring, might have passed for some jungle of the tropics, in whose depths lurked the tawny lion and stealthy panther, ready to spring upon the unwary traveler. Through this sea of verdure, the narrow road wound like a ribbon, following the tortuous course of the stream which grew smaller as it approached the upper end of the valley, and the travelers suddenly paused in rapt admiration at the scene which met their view. Before them lay an open glade covered with short thick turf and dotted here and there with large trees, which so arranged themselves as to form a natural vista, at the upper end of which suspended, as it seemed from the blue dome of heaven, hung a silvery vail delicate as air, and veined with gold and silver, emerald and ruby, pearl and purple; and every glittering splendor as it hung, caught light from some radiance beneath, and flashed its sparkles upon the air till it seemed the jeweled curtain to some enchanted grotto, where the noiads and mermaids danced to the to rhythm of the flowing waters.

Not a word was spoken by the foremost group till they stood upon a huge mass of stone which had fallen from the top of the cliff, and lifted their bared heads to receive the baptism of the spray, then Our Artist drew a deep sigh of enjoyment, and said in a half whisper—

"I never realized the beauty of water before. It reminds me of a description I read not long ago of the bottom of the sea—I only remember a few lines. "When the shadows of night spread in the deep waters, the exquisite garden which they cover is lighted up with new splendors. The medusæ and the microscopic crustacians shine in the bottom like fairy stars;

the pennatula floats in a phosporescent light; every corner of the sea-bottom sends out its ray of color; and to complete the marvels of this enchanted night scene, the large silver disk of the moon-fish moves safely through the whirling vortices of little stars."

"That description is beautiful enough to make us all desire to become divers of the 'vasty deep'," said the Historian as her voice ceased. "I would like to see this scene by moonlight, but, unfortunately, the new moon is yet too young for its light to penetrate to this deep vale."

"You had better say it is a *fortunate* thing for us poor feminines," said Cap, for I am morally sure if any of you lords of creation were to propound a certain question to me on this rock, by moonlight, I should be obliged to say yes whether I wanted to or not. So I am glad I shall not be tempted to make any of you miserable for life."

"As usual, Cap has found the step from the sublime to the ridiculous and this time she has assistance down the declivity," said Aunt Quimby, pointing to a group on the bank of the creek behind them, consisting of a man and two women, who seated with their backs to the cataract were composedly dipping snuff from the same black bottle, while near by a single ox, attached to a white-topped wagon, grazed leisurely around.

"I do not believe *they* would consider the subject of love ridiculous, for I think they must be on their bridal tour," said Meg Merrilles. "I cannot imagine what else can have brought them so far from 'the busy haunts of men, and they all, the ox included, have rather a sheepish look."

I begin to believe with Bryant that if one could

> "Take the wings
> Of the morning, and the Barcan desert pierce;
> Or lose HIMSELF in the continuous woods
> Where rolls the Oregon,"

he would still meet creatures of his kind," said Rashleigh Obaldstone. "Five minutes ago I did not believe there was a human being within a circuit of five miles of this place except ourselves, and now those people look as if they might have been here ever since the mountains were created. Miss Die, let's climb this mountain, and see if we cannot discover—

> "Some fairy shore
> Where mortals never trod before."

"Some enchanted isle

> "Where not a pulse should beat but YOURS,
> And YOU might live, love, die alone,"

I suppose," quoted the irrepressible Cap, as the twain moved off arm in arm. "Mr. Historian, let's you and I be the serpents to invade this

—Paradise so pure and lonely."

This was agreed to, and Aunt Quimby and Lord Chesterfield persuaded to join them in attempting the ascent of the mountain, while the rest of the party preferred returning by the way they had come.

Just at the fall, the mountain presented a perpendicular front of 180 feet, which defied all attempts to scale it; but a few yards to the left the ascent was less precipitous, and they soon struck into a narrow path which wound up towards the top. Capitola and the Historian, the madcaps of the party, soon distanced the other walkers, though the steepness of the ascent after a time, caused even their fleet footsteps to flag, and they paused on a projecting point to draw breath, look and laugh at the laborious ascent of their companions. Die being "fair and fat," if not forty, weighed about a hundred and fifty pounds, and it required Rashleigh's full strength to pull her up the mountain; while Aunt Quimby and Lord Chesterfield, neither of whom possessed much ponderosity, were constantly being thrown out of the path by roots and stones, and several times came near toppling over the precipice.

"Mr. Historian has been congratulating himself that I was 'a spare made gal,' as our North Carolina friend used to say," said Cap, as the panting couple reached them. "Sir Rashleigh wishes that you were one too, Die, I expect, though he may think with Azim—

"These steeps, though dark and dread,
Heaven's pathways if to thee they led."

"I think we have misnamed *you*," said Die, as soon as she could catch her breath. "You ought to have been called a 'Walking Dictionary of Poetical Quotations,' and I suspect you have been doing as Falstaff wished to do before starting on the trip, cramming for this and all other probable and improbable occasions. But your arrows, however double headed, generally miss their mark.

"See that they do not yet find the joints in your harness," retorted Cap, provoked at the sarcastic tone which pointed her words, and taking the Historian's arm they resumed their upward way, and were soon at the top.

Meanwhile the sun had climbed to its meridian height, and the thin clouds that veiled its face only tempered but did not extinguish the warmth of its rays, so that the pedestrians were glad to rest awhile on the top of the mountain, though there was little to repay them for the fatigue of their walk.

The stream which till now had crept through the landscape with so little width or depth as scarcely to merit the title of creek, had here, at the brow of the mountain, fallen among breakers, and after chafing and fretting at them for a few yards, made its escape by leaping over the precipice into the valley beneath, with a velocity so great in proportion to its volume that before it reached the ground each drop separated into minute particles, that hung suspended in the air like a lace vail with designs richer far than any loom of Brussels or Valenciennes ever produced. But from their present position at the top of the mountain, the beauties of the cataract were invisible, and looking down, the eye saw nothing but the tops of the trees below, which seemed to fill the valley to overflowing; while on the hills around serried ranks of these giants of the wood seemed keeping solemn guard over their brethren in the valley beneath.

The smooth rocks edging the stream were thickly inscribed with the initials of adventurous tourists, but our travelers, remembering the adage in regard to fool's names and faces, contented themselves with inscribing theirs upon small detached portions of slate and wood which they exchanged among themselves as mementoes of the trip; then, when the gentlemen had with some difficulty formed a bridge of poles over the stream, they crossed and made all the haste they could to rejoin their companions on the other side of the valley.

They reached the road over which they had come at a point above that at which they had left the carriages, and while wondering at the non-appearance of their companions, they were startled by a succession of shrieks from the valley beneath. Wild stories of adventures with Indians and wild beasts, blanched the cheeks of the ladies, while the Historian rushed down the hill with such haste that before reaching the bottom he fell and accomplished the balance of the distance by a series of somersets, which at length landed him in the midst of a laughing group which enclosed Lady Montague, and the front wheels of the double buggy.

This good lady, while attempting to drive herself and children up the hill in this vehicle, suddenly found herself, by the breakage of the coupling pin, dragged over the dash-board, and following the horse and front wheels up the hill, while the children, so unceremoniously left behind with the body and hind wheels, uttered doleful screams. After a few seconds Lady Montague succeeded in stopping the horse, and picking herself up, found she was unhurt, and was ready to laugh with the rest as her awkward mishap. The Historian's ready knife soon repaired the damage by whittling out a wooden pin, and they were all soon stored away in the carriages, and with many promises of a week's sojourn among these romantic scenes when they had more time, bade a lingering farewell to Tocoa.

CHAPTER XV.

The trip back to Clarksville was rather a silent one for several miles, each seeming to be occupied with his own thoughts, the silence only broken now and then by inquiries about the distance from both the gentlemen and ladies, all of whom began to have a realizing sense that the dinner hour was long since past, and no eatables were to be had any nearer than Clarksville, while the road seemed to lengthen interminably.

"A penny for your thoughts, Don Quixote," at length exclaimed Cap, whose nimble tongue had really been still for some minutes.

"They are worth far more than a penny," he responded gallantly, "for I was thinking of you."

"Oh, what nice things you do say," she replied with a comical nod of her head. "But do let us know your thoughts, for I know they must have been profound with so weighty a subject as myself."

"I was only wondering what made you so quiet, and was about to beg you to—

"Cast that shadow from thy brow,
My dark-eyed love be glad again"—

interrupted the Historian in a pretended aside to Die, who nodded approvingly at this fighting the enemy with her own weapons.

Cap's only answer to this thrust was a contemptuous shrug of her shoulders, as she turned to Don Quixote.

"I was quiet because, as an old friend of mine used to say, I feel to sympathize with the crow, who 'had no grub to ate,'" and without waiting for any response, she gave out the first two lines of "The Three Black Crows," and raised it to a tune whose ludicrous solemnity set them all to laughing, though they joined in the air; Miss Patty singing high trible in a manner irresistibly comic.

"Who shall say I am not a magician, when I have succeeded for half an hour in making three of the 'lords of creation' forget that they have had no dinner, and amusing them when they were hungry?" exclaimed Cap. as the spires of Clarksville came in view. "Gentlemen, I think I deserve a vote of thanks from you all."

"We will pay you in something more substantial when we reach the town," said the Historian, and, true to his promise, when they paused in the public square to ascertain the whereabouts of Falstaff, he disappeared, but soon returned laden with ginger-cakes baked in the shape of hearts, which he distributed among them. They were all too hungry to be fastidious, and the merriment that these unique specimens of art gave rise to attracted the attention of a group of idle loungers on a corner, who stared so impudently, that the gentlemen gave the signal for the cortege to move on to the upper end of the village, where they had learned that Falstaff had procured rooms in the house of a lady who was in the habit of accommodating parties of tourists.

Here the comfort and even elegance of their accommodations made the ladies ashamed of their rough and travel-stained appearance, and learning from Falstaff that they need give themselves no concern about supper, which he had engaged a cook to prepare, they retired to their room to make their appearance more in accordance with their surroundings.

The curious chronicler might record some amusing scenes which took place before the single glass, which alternately reflected dark braids and sunny curls, blue eyes and black, as their different owners made the most of the few arts of the toilet which they had in their possession; but we forbear to intrude upon them at these mysterious rites, further than to note that Mrs. Gummidge and the fair Manolia were observed to take particular pains with their toilets, and, on being questioned, said that one of the gentlemen had promised to bring up two young friends of his from the town to call upon them that evening, and they were afraid they would not be able to make a presentable appearance with the means at their command. The rest being quite content with their present attendants were satisfied to make the best of their limited wardrobes, without spending time in primping, and soon left them to partake of the bounteous supper Falstaff's care had provided; and when they all assembled in the handsomely lighted parlor, no handsomer group need have been wished, for the gentlemen, through respect to their fair companions, had done all they could to remove the traces of the day's rough experience and compared favorably with the two beaux from the village who soon made their appearance, and after being presented to the company were turned over to the two ladies for whom the call was designed, while the rest assembled around the handsome piano at the other end of the long parlor, from which Miss Patty Pace's skillful fingers were soon drawing sweet strains to which the rest kept time with their voices.

This had not progressed very long when it was interrupted by the entrance of a party of young people from the town, acquaintances of the lady of the house, who had come ostensibly to get up a dance, but really to inspect our tourists. Among them was several of the loungers whose bold glances had so annoyed the ladies in the evening, several of them so much under the influence of liquor that, if they had not been guests of their hostess, the gentlemen would have requested them to leave the house; and nothing but respect due the first callers, young lawyers of distinetion and ability, as well as perfect gentlemen, prevented the ladies from leaving the parlor. The quiet dignity of the party, however, soon convinced the intruders that they were in the wrong company, and after singing "Jim, crack corn," and a few other hilarious songs, they took their departure, leaving anything but a favorable impression of the beaux of Clarksville upon the minds of the tourists.

The dawn of another bright summer's morning found the party refreshed by a good night's rest, and eager to turn their faces homeward, though their spirits were saddened by the necessity of parting with a portion of their company whose homes lay in another direction. So close had been the companionship of the past week, that it was like the sundering of family ties for them to separate, and the more tender-hearted of the ladies shed tears when the time for the farewell came, and the family carriage which had joined us near Gainsville disappeared in an opposite direction to the one they were to take; for, after much consultation, the gentlemen of the party had decided to avoid the circuitous route by which they had come, and return by the direct road from Clarksville to Athens.

When they was about to start, it was discovered that the single portion of the party having lost four of its members, the remainder could all ride in the ambulance. In it they were accordingly stowed away with the exception of Falstaff, who once more led the van. The party were naturally too light hearted to remain long depressed, and ere many miles had passed the tide of banter and fun was again in full flow, broken now and then by interludes of serious talk, or snatches of favorite melodies, all of which made the time fly so rapidly that when a motion was made for dinner it was vetoed by the majority; most of whom, now that the excitement of sightseeing was over, were eager to reach home. The horses, however, began to show signs of weariness, and it was decided to stop to feed them at the first convenient place.

A well by the road side, situated in a grove whose dense shadows woed the travelers to rest, soon presenting itself, the horses were unharnessed and bountifully supplied with food; but an inspection of the provision trunk brought to light the fact that the bipeds of the party were likely to go unprovided for, as a small quantity of corn meal was the sole remnant of the bountiful supplies with which they had started. Rather long faces greeted this aspect of affairs, especially among the gentlemen, and after a whispered consultation between Lady Montague and Mrs. Gummidge, they disappeared in the direction of a farm house near by, and, after a short absence, returned with a tray, sifter and oven with which they set to work, and with the assistance of the negro drivers soon made and baked some large pones of bread, which with a bucket of fresh milk, and plenty of butter was pronounced by the gentlemen to be a repast fit for a king. The ladies also did ample justice to the meal with the exception of Capitola who retained her seat in the ambulance, declaring she never intended to scratch her throat by attempting to swallow corn bread, especially when baked in the form of "steel pone," and served on a work bench. Her quips and witticisms on their appearance as they surrounded the rustic table, was the sauce which seasoned the informal meal, and when it was over, and *en avant* was once more the cry, it was found that the Historian was about to repay her for the loss of her dinner by a ride in Falstaff's buggy, the latter having good humoredly resigned his place in it for a seat in the ambulance. As he was a great favorite with all the young people, they made room for him eagerly, but the afternoon proved so warm that even *his* quaint jokes and jolly good humor failed to stir the party into much life, till the conversation accidentally turned upon the associations connected with names, when Miss Patty suddenly roused up and electrified them all by propounding an entirely new theory. She said that every name suggested to her some tangible object; some sounding like pieces of flannel, others like rocky roads, or rolls of dough, and so on *ad libitum*. Amid the bursts of laughter which this unique idea provoked, each enquired what his name sounded like, and, unabashed by the general ridicule, she with the utmost gravity, and without the slightest hesitation mentioned different objects, most of which were so utterly remote from anything likely to be suggested by her surroundings, that they all stared at her in utter amazement; and on her telling Roscius that his name sounded like a green glass bottle, Falstaff took the privilege of an old friend to beg her never to advance such ideas again, or people would think her a monomaniac. But she only laughed and called upon Lady Montague to prove that she had often heard her say such things before, and, therefore, they were not manufactured for the occasion. That good lady not only confirmed what Miss Patty had said, but confessed that she too must plead guilty to a similar hallucination, if such it might be termed, only names suggested *colors* instead of *objects* to her. The merriment which such a confession from one of the elders of the party provoked, lasted till near sunset, when they suddenly emerged from the woods in front of a farm house whose surroundings bespoke a rough plenty that decided Falstaff to make it a stopping place for the night, if lodging could be procured.

The house had originally been a one story log building of two rooms, but had expanded to suit the wants of the growing family, till it reminded the observers of a warty squash, so numerous and irregular were the excresences that projected from every part of it; but, unsightly as these were in an architectural point of view, they gave promise of roomy accommodations for our travelers; and an application to the owner of the house, a pleasant-faced widow, resulted in their taking possession of three rooms, which however bare of adornment, were well supplied, with the most essential requirement to our weary travelers—clean, neat looking beds. The party were so much fatigued that most of them went regularly to bed in ten minutes after getting into the house, but Aunt Quimby, whose little frame possessed a wonderful degree of elasticity, and who, like Martha, was apt to be "troubled about many things," now felt such a realizing sense that outside the house were seven hungry masculines whose supper would not prepare itself, that she could not compose herself to sleep; and after a short talk with Cap, who was as usual wide awake when all the rest were sleepy, the two stole off, and finding that the lady of the house possessed the luxury of a cooking stove, went to work and by dark had ready an appetizing meal of egg-bread, scrabbled eggs and hot coffee, to which even the sleepy ones did not refuse to do justice, and found themselves so much refreshed thereby that the most of them acceded to Falstaff's wish that they should adjourn to the porch and have some music. The moonlight lay upon the earth like molton silver, giving its own charm to the rude surroundings, and inspirited by its influence they sang solos, glees and choruses that awoke strange echoes among the encircling woods, till the Queen of Night, rising high in her orbit, warned them of the necessity of retiring.

Adjoining the room which had been appointed to the ladies was a small room containing one bed, which had not been included in the part allotted to the travelers, but, finding it unoccupied at bedtime, and the beds in their room being already filled to overflowing, Die and Meg determined to take possession of it, and have one uninterrupted night's rest. About midnight, Meg was waked by finding Die's head on her pillow with her lips to her ear, begging her in a tremulous whisper to wake up and see who was in the room. Sure enough the outer door, communicating with the porch, stood wide open, and shoes which had a masculine creak, were passing about the room. The girls held on to each other in breathless suspense, fearing they scarcely knew what, till they heard the footsteps ascending the staircase to the room above, and the fall of a heavy pair of boots told the intruder was preparing for bed. Then they drew a long breath of relief, remembering that their hostess had warned them not to be alarmed if they heard a noise in the house, as her sons and daughters were gone to a party from which they would not return till late, and the young man had passed through the room without knowing it was occupied. The girls did not slumber very soundly after this, and rose with the sun to make preparations to follow Lady Montague, who had left with her children to take breakfast with a relative that lived in the neighborhood.

A cold breakfast was partaken of hurriedly, for a journey of forty miles lay between them and the homes which they hoped to reach that night, and by seven o'clock they had overtaken Lady Montague who had arrived safely at her destination. She had not, however, finished her breakfast, so that the party halted to wait for her, and at the same time partake of some fine fruit.

CHAPTER XVI.

It was after eight o'clock when they were once *en route*, then the day promised to be so warm, that Falstaff enjoined a slow rate of travel as the only means of making their horses stand the journey which lay before them. As the party were once more on familiar ground, he resigned his buggy to the young people of the party, and took his place in the ambulance on the plea that the party no longer needed a pioneer, but more than one believed it was to be near Meg whose bright eyes had bewitched him, and the sly jokes and glances which his solicitude for her comfort excited, kept them all amused for sometime.

As the day grew warmer, however, conversation languished, and all seemed inclined to meditation till a sudden lurch of the ambulance sent Aunt Quimby's memorandum book from its place in the top of the ambulance into the lap of the Historian.

"Why have we not thought of this before," he exclaimed. "This will be our last chance of a peep into the contents of this wonderful volume, so do Aunt Quimby enliven us this morning with another one of your stories."

This was eagerly seconded by all the party, and after some demurring she opened the book, and after looking over its pages for some time said:

"I find I have exhausted the memoranda of my first visit to Georgia, but I can read a story the material for which I collected during a second visit which I made here during the war and without further preface she began

THE SORGHUM BOILING.

Reader, did you ever attend a sorghum boiling? I am afraid you are unacquainted with that pleasure especially if the lines have fallen unto you in any other place than Dixie. Even General Sherman in the frequent trips he made through the late Confederacy did not become fully acquainted with the saccharine fluid, for, after flooding half the cellars in Macon with it, he turned to a citizen who stood by gazing at the destruction and pointing to the flowing syrup said:—"You call that sor— sor— *sorghum*, do you not?" "Yes," meekly responded the man. "Well, I wish you Secesh to find something better to stock your cellars with before I come again, for that compound does not suit my palate. In spite of the disapproval of so famous a person I will venture to write a few words about Sorghum—a plant which a kind Providence seemed to send especially to supply some of the necessities of the Southern people during the sufferings of the late war. And for fear some dainty belle, who knows nothing of the war except that it furnishes material for the dilightful sensation stories which she devours so eagerly, may not know what I am talking about, I will give you a brief description of the plant.

It is a species of sugar-cane, not confined to tropical latitudes but growing readily in any temperate climate from ten to fifteen feet in height, and ripening in October. It seems especially designed for man when in extremity, for every part of the plant is useful. Not only is the juice, when boiled, an excellent substitute for molasses, but the fodder is equal to that gathered from corn; the seed, of which it yields about fifty bushels to an acre, when ground makes an eatable bread, and unrivalled chop for horses, while the stalks after being crushed in the mill, form an excellent food for all animals save those of a ruminating kind, which it is apt to kill by swelling in the upper stomach. So much for the nature and uses of sorghum, and for fear you are beginning to think this matter of fact article more suitable for a Patent Office Report, or book of statistics, than the columns of a magazine, I will try to extract some romance even from this unromantic subject, and to do, so I must tell you of a Sorghum Boiling I attended down in Georgia.

It was a breezy October morning with just enough frost in the air to make it bracing and healthy. The distant forest, like a modest nymph, had retired behind a curtain of mist to don her autumnal robes of purple and gold, but the gorgeous colors broke through the thin veil, now and then, betraying the beauty behind. The river at the foot of the lawn sparkled and danced on its way through the fields just beginning to assume the russet hues of "the saddest season of the year," while from the village on the opposite bank the smoke curled gracefully towards the deep blue sky, and the merry shouts of the children at play came pleasantly to the ear.

Breakfast was over at "Myrtle Hill," as the Hyliard plantation was called, and a merry party had gathered on the colonade to enjoy the fresh air for awhile before dispersieg for the day's duties and employments. Archie Hilyard was sketching a ludicrous caricature on one of the pillars, and had called Lucy Douglas to look at it, a summons she had readily obeyed, glad of any excuse to be near the one to whom she had given the first pure love of her youthful heart. His sister Lizzie had gone without invitation, and stood peering over her brother's shoulder laughing merrily at the amateur performance.

Rosa Harris, conscious of looking her best in a white wrapper worn with special reference to Charley Hilyard's taste, had accepted his invitation to see him feed his hounds, and now stood at the foot of the steps patting and fondling the huge creatures, though I knew each uncouth gambol sent her heart into her mouth, for she was naturally timid.

I, plain Annie Leigh, being unceremoniously left out in the grouping, stood with my back to the rest of the party endeavoring to persuade myself that I was enjoying the thousand beauties of field and forest outspread before me, but conscious of a great pain at my heart which I strove in vain to still.

I had known the Hilyards from my earliest childhood; for many years our parents had lived on adjoining estates, and when five years before a malignant fever swept away my father and mother in the short space of one week, their hospitable doors were thrown open, and the poor orphan girl received as one of their own family. There I remained until the first shock of grief had passed, and I was able to look the future in the face. I was alone in the world, except a few distant relations, who were unable or unwilling to assist me, and who would have considered their wealth and pride contaminated by contact with my poverty, for my father's affairs were found to be involved, his creditors were repacious, and when all was settled I was penniless and homeless; even the old homestead endeared by childish pleasures and maturer joys, had passed away to strangers. The Hilyards urged me to remain with them, but I had too much just pride to remain dependent on those upon whom I had no claim. There was then nothing left to me but teaching, the one path which seems open to women reared as I had been; and for this position I was well fitted by the superior education it had been my father's pride to bestow on his only child, without the thought that it would one day be her only means of support.

Finding me firm in my determination to support myself, Mr. Hilyard succeeded in procuring me a situation in a city seminary. With fear and trembling, for I was a sad coward about venturing on untried duties, I entered my new sphere. In it I had been more successful than I had dared to hope, for I had retained the situation, and for ten months out of the twelve I trod daily the same treadmill round, my weary feet, and fainting heart, upheld by a strong will, and the knowledge that my two month's respite would be spent with the Hilyards, who always claimed me as soon as school duties were over. How blessed seemed the quiet and repose of their country home to my tired frame, worn and weary of the din and bustle of my city home. What stores of pleasant memories I gathered up to cheer me in my long exile from them, and how I looked and longed for this one oasis in my barren existence, none may know, but those who have trod the same path—the rough causeway of a teacher's life.

Living thus for many days in constant intercourse with Charley Hilyard, the recipient of so many kind attentions, and realizing in him my ideal of manly perfection, it is not wonderful that admiration, gratitude and esteem became merged into a more enduring passion, but this I would not acknowledge even to my own heart, till Charley went to California two years before, from whence he had only returned at the beginning of the war. During his absence we had corresponded, and, though his letters were only such as a brother might have written to a well beloved sister, I welcomed their arrival as the greatest events of my life, and almost unconsciously to myself, they became the foundation of many a day dream and airy vision so fair and beautiful that they imparted some of their own bright hues to the dull and unromantic present.

On his return he had called to see me in my city home. We met in the common parlor of my boarding house, and the presence of others, as well as the remembrance of the thoughts I had been indulging, embarrassed me, and rendered me unable to respond in a cordial manner to his frank expressions of pleasure at seeing me. He could only spare me a few minutes, for he was hasteening home to see the dear ones from whom he had been so long separated, and they were spent in awkward attempts at conversation, for my constraint had soon communicated itself to him, and it was with a feeling of relief that I saw the interview terminate which I had anticipated so long, and so joyously. It was many months ere I saw him again, for he soon after joined the army and was ordered to Virginia.

This summer, for the first time, I hesitated to go to the Hilyards. While I was still debating the question, I received a letter from a maiden aunt of my father's, who, finding her health declining, suddenly remembered the niece whom she could now make useful, and wrote begging me to come to her. For a few moments my heart rebelled against thus yielding to the demands, and giving up my holiday to one who had neglected me in my lonely orphanage, but I said over to myself the precept taught me in my early childhood by my mother, "Recompense not evil for evil, but do good to those who dispitefully use you," and I decided to go. Perhaps I was helped to this determination by the knowledge that Charley Hilyard was at home disabled by a severe wound in the hand, for the weakness of my heart taught me to avoid one whom I believed felt no warmer affection for me than friendship. I could not pray each day "not to be lead into temptation," and then wilfully place myself where the peace for which I was striving would be endangered every hour; so at the last moment, so as to allow no time for remonstrances from her, I wrote to Lizzie apprising her of my change of plan, and took the cars for my aunt's residence in an adjoining State.

Lizzie's answer was full of reproaches, telling how much they were all disappointed, and declaring that Charley had done nothing but mope since the receipt of my letter. Her next mentioned the arrival of a cousin whom they had not seen for years—a Miss Rosa Harris, a Kentucky Belle; and her subsequent letters were full of the amusements they were getting up for the entertainment of their guest, who would remain with them till the winter.

It was a trial to turn from these delightful pictures of country life and pleasures to the darkness and stillness of the sick room, where pills and powders reigned supreme; but I remained firm at my post. About the time my vacation was over, my aunt died. I believe my presence was a great comfort to her in her last hours, and this helped me to bear the disappointment when her will was read, leaving her property to a distant relative, who already had a superfluity. I had not worked for pay, and did not now repine, though, enfeebled as I was by nursing, I was in no fit condition to resume my school duties. However, "necessity knows no law," and a few days found me back in my old orbit pursuing the same dull routine. But worn out nature revenged herself, and ere many weeks I I was stricken down with a severe attack of fever.

At the first intelligence of my illness, Mrs. Hilyard and Lizzie had hastened to my bedside. They nursed me with untiring care, and as soon as I was declared convalescent, bore me off, unheeding my remonstrances, to their home. Charley came for us, and if I had never loved him before, I must have been won by the tender assiduity, and thoughtful care he manifested for my comfort on the journey.

"At "Myrtle Hill I found Rosa Harris, and though no one could help rendering the meed of admiration to her beauty and grace, there seemed an instinctive repulsion between us at our first meeting, and farther acquaintance rather increased than diminished this feeling. I felt her to be a cold, heartless, world-wedded coquette; while she looked down from a height of immeasurable superiority upon the plain, insignificant teacher. Thus matters stood on the morning I have introduced the family group to the reader.

Archie's picture progressed rapidly amidst the laughter of the girls, and Rosa and Charley still lingered at the foot of the steps apparently in a confidential *tete a-tete*, when Nettie

Hilyard danced out on the colonade with an open note in her hand exclaiming gaily:

"Oh! girls, here is a prospect for another frolic! Mrs. Mitchel has written inviting us to her Sorghum Boiling."

"It will be rather a doubtful sort of fun if we have the work to do," said Lizzie, "unless you are fonder of being stuck up than I am."

"Oh! you don't understand! Listen to what she writes to Mamma," and she read aloud from the note she held in her hand:

DEAR MRS. HILYARD:

Our Sorghum has turned out remarkably well—we have barreled about five hundred gallons. This is the last day of the boiling, and the girls, have determined to invite some young people, and end with a frolic. Your family must be sure to come this evening, and bring any guests they may have with them.

Yours,

M. MITCHELL.

"Ah! it is a 'lasses lickin,' as they say out here" said Archie. "Miss Anna, were you ever at one?"

I shook my head and asked what a "lasses lickin'" was.

"Oh! we, Virginians, would call it a 'candy-stew,' or "taffy-pulling," he replied laughing. "The Georgians have coined a new name, and call them "lasses likins"

"We must be sure to go," said Lucy Douglass, "for I have a great curiosity to see how such things are conducted out here. A few days ago a young lady was describing to me the amusements in her neighborhood last winter, and she said they had a number of 'lasses lickins' up in her 'beat' at which they had "lots of taffy and goobers" and "a powerful sight of fun."

"What are you all discussing up there," called out Charley Hilyard, as the laugh subsided. "Cousin Rosa, shall we go up and see what's to pay?" and he offered his arm to assist her up the steps. She accepted it, and sauntering carelessly up to the group, encircled me with her arm.

I shuddered involuntarily at her touch, and it was only by an effort that I restrained the impulse to free myself from the seemingly affectionate clasp, for I knew this novel display of affection for one towards whom she had never shown ought but cool indifference, was to serve some purpose of her own; and I shrank from the comparison I felt Charley must be drawing as we stood thus together in front of him. Heaven knows I did not envy her beauty, though that was as brilliant as raven hair, faultless features, and a queenly carriage could make it, but I *did* envy her the possession of Charley Hilyard's heart, which I believed she had won from me,

The subject under discussion was explained and the note read again.

"We must all go," said Charley, "for I want one more good frolic before I go back to camp—it may be long enough before I have another. I wonder who will be there? Mr. Meredeth, of course, for one."

"Oh! yes, and Miss Anna must certainly go," said Rosa, Harris, turning to me. "One more meeting will bring him to the proposal point, and end the matter 'favorably.'"

"Is that a consumation devoutly to be hoped for, Miss Anna?" said Charley, with a quick glance at me.

"Of course it is," she said quickly without giving me time to answer. "Miss Anna is much too sensible a woman to allow such an eligible chance of a settlement in life escape her. I think it will suit admirably, for we all know Miss Anna's prediliction for a country life, and Mr. Meredith was telling us the other day how much he needed a house-keeper, and lamenting that his children were growing up with no better care than that of the servants. I feel sorry for him."

"Ah! it is to be a *marriage de convenence* then on both sides? Miss Anna I had thought would never be influenced by such motives, but I am beginning to believe that what has been said of men is true of women—"they all have their price."

He spoke with some bitterness, and I opened my lips to defend myself, but closed them again firmly, saying within myself, "If the words of an idle trifler like she can shake the opinion formed by years of intimate companionship, let it be so; but the pang at my heart gave a kneen satire to my tone as I turned to Rosa Harris, who was surveying me with a look of mocking derision:

"Miss Harris feels so much amiable sympathy for Mr. Meredith that I think she had better try to ameliorate his forlorn condition by taking him herself. The motives she ascribes to me would be much more consonant with *her* feeling than mine, and I am not yet so much reduced as to be obliged to hire myself out as house-keeper or nursery maid;" and with a mocking bow I walked to the other end of the colonade.

Charley followed me in a few minutes to ask at what time we should start on the daily ride which had been prescribed by the physician, and which he had been careful to give me every day of my convalescence.

I declined taking it to-day, saying my health was now restored, and I stood in no further need of such prescriptions.

"Is restored health any reason why you should deny me a pleasure?" he asked gently.

"No; but a very *good* reason why I should relieve you of a troublesome duty," I answered coldly.

"I thought you knew ere this, Anna, that nothing I can do for you is a trouble;" he said in a reproachful tone. "But I suppose you must have decided to change your escort, as I see Mr. Meredith coming? Must I believe the report of your intention to marry him, Miss Anna?"

"Believe whatever you choose," I said haughtily, indignant that he should thus continue to tease me, and turning away I entered the house without giving him a chance to say more.

From the window of my room I saw Mr. Meredith's buggy drive up, and fearing he might ask for me, I snatched a bonnet and ran down stairs.

As I passed through the hall, I heard Rosa Harris' splendid voice soaring and swelling in rich volumes of sound as she sang some difficult opera air, and through the half open door of the parlor, caught a glimpse of Charley bending over her in wrapt admiration and devotion. Stung almost to madness by the sight, I flew out of the house and across the lawn to the river bank; breathlessly I climbed the cliffs, unheeding the bushes and briars that impeded my way, till I reached a high point untenanted save by a few goats and their kids belonging to the factory village.

Once in my aerie and I was safe. Above me was the blue sky, beneath a roaring cataract, where the river, shut in by hanging cliffs, dashed precipitately over an immense ledge of rock with a roar that shook the rock upon which I stood. What should hinder me from casting myself down from that dizzy height into the dark and seething pool beneath the fall, and thus ending a life that was alike worthless to myself and others? Who was there in the wide world that my death would grieve?

For a moment I bent over the vortex as these frantic thoughts whirled through my mind, in another, for I was not yet quite crazy, I had thrown myself on my hand and knees, and lifted my hands and eyes in mute supplication towards the Heaven, the laws of whose Righteous Judge I had been tempted to disobey.

After a while the first passionate overflow of feeling subsided, and I sat down, and, pushing back the hair from my face, strove to think calmly. I felt how foolishly I was acting in thus suffering myself to be tossed to and fro on the wild waves of passion, and that too, for one who only thought of me as a sister. Was it not something to have such a brother to trust and depend upon in any difficulty? What was I, poor, homely, obscure, and homeless, save for the shelter their kindness had given me, that I should raise my eyes to one so immeasurable my superior, the heir of that broad domain, caressed and flattered alike by young and old. Our paths in life lay wide apart; his was a flower-strewn way bedecked with honors, mine stretched before me a straight and narrow path of trial, self-denial, and years of loneliness full of the misery which those feel who have nothing for which to live, and only a bitter memory to feed their thoughts upon. And as its full desolation broke upon me, I stretched out my hands in a quick passionate cry for death. The solemn roar of the cataract, not unlike the ceaseless murmur of my own undisciplined heart, was the only sound that answered me, but at that moment I saw on the face of the fall where the water did not quite cover the surface of the rock, a little bird. Undismayed by the boiling waters around it, and the fearful whirlpool beneath, it walked fearfully along, the slippery pathway, occasionally uttering a quick note, seemingly of thanksgiving for its preservation and the mercies of the way. I beheld myself rebuked by one of the least of God's creatures, and felt my own folly in crying out against my fate because the voyage promised to be stormy and boisterous. "I will learn a lesson of thee, little mariner," I said humbly, "I will pursue meekly my way, thankful for any gleam of light that may irradiate its angry billows, securely trusting in the great Pilot who hath promised to bring us into "the haven where we would be;" and as these thoughts arose in my mind, through the soft slumberous air seem to come the command, "Peace, be still," and there was at once a great calm.

Afraid to test my new found composure by an immediate return to the house, I determined to avail myself of the beautiful day to go once more to my old home—a visit which I had been planning secretly ever since learning that the family who had purchased it were away for the summer. It was a short walk of a mile, and descending from my perch, I retraced my steps to the negro cabins where I left a message informing Mrs. Hilyard of my destination, and calling Carlo, the house dog, to follow me, took the well known path over the hills. How often a merry, light-hearted child I had skipped over its well beaten surface! Now, I trod it a woman, my soul heaving with fears and yearnings; but there was a charm still in its well remembered turns, and the familiar land-scape, so peaceful and calm in the rich light of the October sun, crept into my heart filling its desert places with soft comforting calm.

I found but few changes in the old place. The large old trees that had won for it the name of "Wood-lawn" still bowed in as lofty pride over my head as I walked up the avenue an orphan and a stranger, as when I rolled beneath their shadows in a stately carriage, the pet and idol of my parents, and the heiress of that proud estate; and through them the house with its snowy pillars looked out with the aspect of a familiar friend. It is strange how the heart clings to inanimate objects when deprived of other ties! All around me now belonged to another, and had passed away from me, I thought forever, but I felt an ownership of affection in every familiar object, and still mourned for my household gods.

On the colonade steps sat an old woman, who had once belonged to my father, and, being a trusty servant, was in the absence of the mistress, entrusted with the general supervision of the place. She was now busily engaged in kn tting, and watching the movements of a troop of youngsters who were sweeping the yard. At the sight of me she came forward to meet me, dropping a series of old-fashioned curtesies, which at another time and place, might have provoked my laughter. Declining to enter the house in the absence of the owner, I did not refuse the comfortable chair and nice lunch of bread, fruit and milk which Aunt Daphne insisted upon setting out on the colonade for me; and this over I drew the old woman on to speak of the days of which my heart was so full. To this she was no wise averse, for old negroes always feel great pride in relating the traditions of the family in which they have been raised, even though that glory may have departed; and the hours slipped rapidly by in listening to anecdotes of my childhood, intermingled with predictions that those days of comfort and happiness would return and she should live to see me come again to my own; and at which I smiled half in bitterness, half in derision. The lengthening shadows warned me at length, that the short Autumn day was drawing to a close, and it was time for me to retrace my steps towards Myrtle Hill.

"You will go to the grave yard, Mistis, fore you go," said the old woman, as I rose from my seat beside her. "You will see that mammy has not neglected it," she added, as I nodded ascent.

She accompanied me to the gate, then with the instinctive delicacy which makes that class of people understand, and sympathize with sorrows which we never confide to them, she bade me an affectionate good-bye and left me.

All within the enclosure where my parents slept was in exquisite order, showing none of those evidences of neglect which frequently strike the heart so painfully in Southern grave yards. The grass, undisfigured by a single weed, was still green and soft as velvet, and the white tea-rose that stood by the single shaft which marked the double graves was heavy with buds which in a few days would be blossoms. Something in the quiet aspect of the spot seen in the pale lights of evening, touched my heart, and the varied emotions that had been struggling within me found vent in heavy tears as I knelt by the lonely mounds marking the resting place of those guardians of my youth, the memory of whose love, solicitude and care was the one bright spot in memory's waste. Calmer, if not happier, I at length arose and retraced the path I had trodden in the morning. The sun was setting as I reached the hill over-looking the valley in which the Hilyard home lay bosomed in hill and wood, and rising abruptly from the river bank just above the falls whose murmur, softened by the distance, combined pleasantly with the soughing of the wind through the trees above me, the tinkling of distant bells as the cows were being driven home from pasture, and the wild, melancholy cry of the swine-herd which echoed from hill to hill. The shades of twilight were already beginning to gather in the valley, but the house, from its higher situation, still reflected the last rays of the sun, and with its many gleaming windows seemed to have concentrated all the light of the land-scape to itself. A pleasant beacon it looked, guiding the traveler to rest, comfort and hospitality. Oh! how I wished I had the right to claim there for all my future life, a permanent abiding place—a home—magical word in which I should never have right or part, and at the thought the words of one wretched as I now was rushed to my heart and lips—

"Why, why is happiness so brief?
Life's weeds so strong, its flowers so frail?
How mutable the world appears
Where nothing lasts but pain and tears!"

I lingered till the sun disappeared behind the hills, then turned towards the house. As I neared the gate I saw a group on the colonade, and among them recognized several gentlemen and ladies from the neighborhood. Not wishing to meet them just then, I turned into a winding path in the shrubbery leading to a side door, and through that made my escape to my room. Lizzie's foot was soon heard upon the stairs, and she entered full of chidings for my long absence, but before I could answer her a bell rang sharply below.

"There is the tea-bell, and you are not near ready," she exclaimed, "Mamma insisted upon our taking supper before we went to the party, and there is a house full of company here, so I must run down. Make haste and come down, for it is nearly time for us to start."

In spite of her injunction, I lingered over my toilet until I heard the murmur of voices returning from the supper-room. I watched at the head of the stairs, till they were safe in the parlor, then slipped down hoping to find no one in the dining-room but Mrs. Hilyard; but when I entered the room Charley was still standing by the fire.

"How do you do, runaway?" he said coming forward to meet me with extended hand.

I gave him only the tips of my fingers, for I felt they were icy cold, but he persisted in drawing my whole hand into his warm clasp, and led me up to his mother who still sat at the head of the table.

"Mamma, here is the culprit. I hope you will make her fully aware of the enormity of her conduct in thus leaving your house for a whole day without asking your permission. As counsel for the prosecution I would suggest a straight jacket, and solitary confinement for a week on bread and water."

His mother smiled, and passing her arm around me gave me a kind, motherly kiss, which, in my present state of feeling, brought tears to my eyes. Charley seemed to detect my emotion, for he immediately seated me at the table, declaring I must be half starved, and must eat such a supper as Ned Brace did on his trip to Savannah; dispatched half a dozen servants for as many different things, built a fortification of dishes around my plate, and kept the room in such an uproar by his jokes and contradictory orders that it was impossible not to be amused, and I soon found myself laughing merrily, while the knot in my thought rapidly melted away.

"Bravo! I could not have done better myself," said Charley, as I arose from the table. "I am sure after that supper you will be able to go with"——

The sentence, whatever its import, was interrupted by Rosa Harris, who entered the room and without noticing me ran up to Charley exclaiming: "Cousin Charley, it always makes me dreadfully sick to ride in a close carriage. Will you take me over in your open buggy to Mrs. Mitchell's?"

A shadow crossed his face, but he answered in the affirmative. "Oh! that is a dear, good cousin," she exclaimed laying her hand upon his arm, and raising her beautiful eyes sparkling with pleasure to his.

I did not wonder that his face softened, and flushed with admiration as he gazed at her. She was the very style of woman that effects men like draughts of old wine, producing temporary madness and delirium; and, like that, leaving nothing but evil effects behind.

Had Rosa Harris been a true, earnest, good woman, one calculated to lead her husband into paths of righteousness and peace by the gentle iufluenc of her pure life, I think I could have borne, however bitter the trial, to see her win Charley Hilyard; but, knowing, as I did, that her grace, beauty and splendid accomplishments, were but the outside polish—the veneering that covered a poor mind, and coarse nature, jealously, cruel as the grave, gnawed at my heart. Perhaps, something of this feeling was expressed in my features, for after a few moments she turned to me with a triumphant light gleaming in her eyes.

"I hope I am not interrupting any previous arrangement," she said. "Miss Anna has been so romantic and sentimental to-day, prefering "the boundless contiguity of shade" to civilized society, that I am ignorant of her arrangements about going to the party?"

"I have made none that will in the slightest degree interfere with any of yours," I said haughtily.

"I shall return for Miss Anna, if she will permit me," said Charley.

"Do not trouble yourself to do so," I answered coldly, for with Rosa Harris' presence the cloud had returned. "I shall go in the carriage with your mother, if she will allow me?" I added turning to her.

"Certainly, my dear," she said kindly. It will be best for you not to expose yourself to the night air. So you all hurry along and send the carriage back for us."

They obeyed her; and, though the distance was short, it was nearly dark before we started.

"Did you know, my dear, that Charley had an idea of buying Woodlawn?" asked Mrs. Hilyard when we were at last on the road."

"I was thankful for the darkness which concealed my start of surprise.

"Mr. Hanley talks of selling," continued the good lady, unheeding my silence, "and it would suit him very well, for there is no finer estate in the country. We are, of course, anxious for him to settle near us when he marries, which will probably be before long, and this place will suit us all around; for Archie will have the Brent place, Lizzie the Upland Track at her marriage, and Mr. Hilyard is anxious to buy a place for Charley, so that at our deaths we can leave the home place to Annie; and if he can buy Woodlawn they will all be settled near together."

So Rosa Harris would be mistress of the place each foot of which was hallowed to me by precious memories. Truly the waters of a full cup were being wrung out to me, and if the draught had needed bitterness before, it now overflowed. I could not trust my voice to utter a single word, and Mrs. Hilyard, having apparently exhausted all she had to say, leaned back in silence, which was not broken till we reached our destination.

Lights were glancing from window to window, and the merry hum of voices from parlor and colonade, told that the company were already assembled. We were met at the door by one of the young ladies of the house and shown into a back chamber to lay aside our wrappings. The pallid face and gleaming eyes which the mirror revealed to me, seemed ill fitting to a festal gathering; and, for the first time in my life, I sought aid of the adventitious arts of the toilet, but the powder boxes and rouge bottles, relics of better times, which were on the toilet were alike empty, and composing my features as well as I could, I descended, hoping my appearance might be attributed to my recent illness.

In the parlor we found a mingling of young and old, grave and gay. Madame DeStael has said that men only resemble each other when sophiscated by sordid or fashionable life, and that it is only in a state of nature they differ; and the war seemed to prove the truth of these remarks, especially in the Confederacy. Long established customs were overthrown, the behests of Dame Fashion set aside or reduced to the simplest principles, and had some devotee of fashion, fresh from the gayeties of the Shoddy circles of the North been suddenly transported to a "Confederate" party, he would have thought himself in a foreign land, so unique and various would have been the costumes around him; and if, as some suppose, diversity of dress promises equally novel ways of feeling and of judgment, the company that filled Mrs. Mitchell's parlor offered a rich field to the curious inquirer into manners and characteristics.

Here a gay belle flourished in a dress which had once been handsome both in style and fabric, but was now disfigured by flounces of another color put on to lengthen it; there a piece of brocade, which had, perhaps, done execution on the person of some fair dame in the days of hair-powder and high-heeled shoes, had been resurrected by one of her descendants and fashioned into a Garabaldi to do duty with a skirt of another color; on one side, a calico dress, which would have been neat, was spoiled by its attempt at ornament in the shape of flounces and ruffles; on the other, the eyes were attracted by a blue dress, yellow belt and pink ribbons on the person of a dashing widow, who had found mourning very unhealthy now that there were so many soldiers about, and had dressed herself out in the odds and ends found in the stores, adding the finishing touch to her costume by a pair of immense cuffs of bleached homespun, cut in points and laced with crimson cords and tassels; and by her side in delightful contrast, a young girl, who eschewing coarse finery appeared in a homespun of a plain gray color, neatly made, but entirely without ornament, save a bow of bright hued ribbon fastening the simple collar from which the fresh, young face arose, only sweeter and brighter from its plain surroundings, as the purest gem shines brightest from the plainest setting.

Amidst these *bizarreries* of costume Rosa Harris in her fleecy muslin, cherry ribons and brilliant roses in her hair and bosom, reigned a queen, attracting much attention from the uniforms, a score of whom brightened the room, having been collected from a regiment camped in the neighborhood. Foremost in her train was Charley, and to none did the beauty more graciously incline, deferring to his opinion on every subject in a manner that must have been very flattering to his vanity; and from my obscure corner I watched his face, every change of which I knew well, marvelling that it continued so calm and unmoved. Soon Col.——, who had known Miss Harris in Kentucky, approached and with a deferential bow Charley surrendered his place by the side of the beauty, unheeding the soft glance that sought to detain him, and wandered idly through the room, exchanging gay greetings with divers merry belles with whom he was a favorite, but attaching himself to none, and seemingly searching for some one. Presently his mother entered, and he went up and asked some question which she seemed to answer in the affirmative, nodding over in the direction of my corner. At that moment supper was announced, and the rising of the company hid their forms.

Feeling disinclined to eat again, I slipped out of a door near me, and, being familiar with the premises from former visits, threw a shawl over my head and ran out to see the Sorghum Boiling.

The work was carried on in a pine grove just back of the orchard in a little miniature dell through which a small stream wound its way to the river. It was a soft, mild night, so calm and still that, as I paused at the stile which separated the grove from the orchard, I heard the factory bell in the village whose circle of lights I could distinguish on a hill about a mile off strike ten, and caught the faint murmur of the falls though they were still more remote. I waited till the echoes of the bell died away, then mounted the stile and a scene of picturesque beauty lay before me.

The moon just rising in the east, threw long lines of quivering light over the open landscape, but could not penetrate the dense shadows of the grove upon the borders of which a shelter had been erected by driving four stakes in the ground and covering the top with plank. At one end was a rough stone chimney, and under it were four large boilers, the largest capable of holding a hundred gallons, filled with the cane in various stages of preparation.

The glare of the fires thrown into brilliant relief by the dark shadows beyond; the mill with its heavy iron rollers and long beam; the long piles of crushed cane, all gave a novel air to the scene, which was heightened by the red glare of the torches borne by the boilers, who with their black and strongly marked features, turbaned heads, and white cotton dresses, stirring the immense cauldrons, brought Macbeth's witches forcibly to mind, and you almost expected to hear them take up the refrain——

"When shall we three meet again?
In thunder, lightning and in rain,
When the hurly burly's done
When the battle's lost and won."

Struck by the artistic blendings of the lights and shadows in the picture before me, I approached nearer and seated myself at the foot of a tree to enjoy it at leisure. But the silence was soon broken by the murmur of voices in the direction of the house, and the whole company poured out in couples from the dining room to see if the candy was done. I kept my seat, trusting to the obscurity and the dark hues of my dress to conceal me from observation. They formed in a group around the kiln, filling the lately quiet scene with gay laughter and merry jests, and many exclamations of "How romantic! How picturesque! How sweet!"—pet expletives which sentimental young ladies bestow alike on a purling stream, and the Falls of Niagara—a well kept flower garden, and the majestic wonders of the mountains.

Last of all came Rosa Harris leaning on Col.—— arm, and in rather an ill humor, as I conjectured from the petulant tones of her voice. This was probably caused by the absence of Charley Hilyard, who was not of the party. He came after some time, and as he passed my hiding place, I heard him ask of his sister, who stood near:—"Lizzie, have you seen Miss Anna lately? She was not in the supper room."

"No, I have not," she answered, "but I expect she is at the house with Mamma."

"No, she is not, for I have just come from there. I am afraid she is sick—I noticed how pale she looked when she entered the parlor."

"Oh, do not disturb yourself about her, Cousin Charley," said Rosa Harris in her most sarcastic tones, "I have no doubt she and Mr. Meredith are off somewhere taking a moonlight serenade. That is always the way with these models of propriety."

Just then the candy was pronounced done, and, being poured into dishes and pans, the gentlemen were called upon to assist the servants in carrying it to the house, the girls followed them with the exception of Rosa Harris.

"Shall we go in, Cousin Rosa," said Charley Hilyard approaching her as she stood leaning against a tree.

"No; I have been bored into a headache already," she answered poutingly, "and will stay out here awhile if you will stay with me?"

"Certainly; but are you not afraid of taking cold?"

"Oh! no; I am accustomed to the night air."

"At least, let me get you a shawl," he said gravely.

"Very well; I will wait here till you come back."

He went; and she seated herself at the root of a tree, and leaning back gazed at the moon now riding clear and high in the blue expanse above her. Much as I disliked her, I could but acknowledge the beauty of the face thus revealed in the moonlight. The broad low brow from which the rich brown hair fell in masses of glossy curls, the dazzling brown eyes and full red lips, were all of the fairest order of beauty, and my heart gave a shuddering sigh as I thought whose eyes would soon rejoice in gazing upon the fair picture which she made as she sat there in the moonlight. I arose to steal away, for I had no desire to be a witness of the *tete a tete*, for which she had evidently managed, but a cracking stick betrayed me, and turning her head she saw who it was. She sprung to her feet with a muttered exclamation which sounded like "eavesdropper," gave me one glance of scorn, and walked off towards the house. As she emerged into the full monlight, I saw that her dress was on fire; the flame having crept through the leaves to the place where she had been sitting.

The first impulse of my sore and bitter heart was to say "let her burn." Why should I save one who constantly treats me with scorn and contempt? She must perish ere she can reach other help, and who will know that you saw it?" In that instant I think I realized how a murderess feels. Another and I sprung after her calling her to stop. She glanced back, saw her danger, and wild with fright darted on. Her rapid motion increased the flame which rose rapidly, towards her head. Swiftly as I ran the distance between us seemed to lengthen. At length I overtook her, threw her in spite of her frantic struggles, upon the damp grass, tore off the heavy shawl from my shoulders, enveloped her in it, and had just succeeded in extinguishing the flames when the company, attracted by her screams reached the spot.

I saw Charley Hilyard spring forward and raise her from the ground, and hold her tenderly in his arms while he strove by gentle words to soothe her agitation, which threatened hysterics. On examination her injuries were found to be very slight. Her dress was reduced to cinders, but she was unhurt except a few slight burns on her neck and arms. But the dreadful fate she had just escaped seemed to have made little impression on her, for as soon as the first shock was over she began to mourn over her hair, which was very much scorched and burnt.

"Better thank God that you have been saved from a violent death," said Charley Hilyard in a grave voice, releasing her from his arms.

"I think we are forgetting that there may be another sufferer," said a voice which I recognized as Mr. Meredith's.

Charley came to my side instantly—"Are you hurt Anna?" he asked in a voice which made my heart throb? But I had just seen what I thought his tenderness for Rosa Harris, and answered coldly.

"I believe my hands are a little blistered. I will go to the house and get Mrs. Mitchel to bind them up for me," and I turned away unheeding the compliments of the crowd on my presence of mind; but the movement made me sensible of a violent pain in my ankle, which increased so rapidly that when I reached the stile I was compelled to sit down on the step. The rest of the company had passed on unconscious of my situation for I had made light of my suffering, and rejected their assistance, and as I sat striving to overcome the faintness which oppressed me, a keen sense of neglect and lonliness pierced me and I cried aloud, "Who in all the world thinks of me? Why can I not die?"

"I care for you, Anna, more than words can tell," said a deep voice by my side. "Why do you treat me thus? Why not suffer me to help you?"

The blood, which had forsaken cheek and lips, came back with a rush, but I was too much agitated to speak. He stooped and took my hand, perhaps something in my face, clearly revealed in the moonlight, emboldened him, for in a moment I felt myself raised and held in a clasp that was at once sooting and strengthening; and, finding I was unable to walk, he took me up like a child in his strong arms and bore me to the house, never pausing till he had placed me in his mother's care.

The journey home that night is a dream, for worn out with the excitement I had undergone, and the pain I was suffering from my ancle, which was badly sprained, I was but dimly consciouse of what passed around me.

The next day was spent on a couch by the fire in Lizzie's room in a feverish stupor, half waking, half sleeping, in which my mind, as inert as my body, framed but few thoughts, and was barely conscious of surrounding objects, and the kind offices which Mrs. Hilyard and Lizzie were assiduous in bestowing. Once during the day Rosa Harris came in and stood beside me. I felt her presence by the thrill of repulsion which ran over me, though I did not open my eyes.

"Do you think she will die?" she asked as she looked down at me.

"Oh! no;" said Lizzie who sat by, "it is only the effect of over exertion; she will be better to-morrow."

"I hope so;" she said carelessly, adding a moment after in a tone of chilling condescension—"She seems to be an amiable person, and I am really greatly obliged to her for her efforts in my behalf yesterday."

"You ought to be *deeply grateful* to her, for she saved you from a horrible death," Lizzie answered with some warmth, "and I am sure if you knew her as well as we do, you would love her for her superior qualities of mind and heart."

"Oh! I never had any fancy for superior women, probably because I am such a sinner myself," she answered, and with a toss of her head sailed away.

Lizzie bent over me a moment when she was gone, to ascertain if I was asleep, and my regular breathing deceiving her, she folded my shawl more closely over me, kissed my cheek softly and stole away; and with a gush of thankfulness in my heart for the love she expressed, I fell into a deep sleep which lasted several hours.

The setting sun was gilding the wall when I awoke to find Mrs. Hilyard sitting beside me—"You have had a nice nap, and I am sure you are better," she said as I opened my eyes. "You can eat something now?"

I did feel greatly refreshed, and ate with appetite the food she brought me, the first that had passed my lips that day.

"You are looking so revived by your tea," she said when I finished, "that I think you can receive a visitor. Charley has been worrying about you all day—may he come and sit with you awhile?"

I nodded assent with a flushed cheek, and she went below. In a few minutes I heard his step on the stairs, each foot-fall sending the blood in swift currents to my heart. He came directly to my side, and taking my bandaged hands in his, pressed them to his lips, and there was no need of words in that moment when heart spoke to heart.

"Mamma said I might sit with you till supper if I would not agitate you in any way;" he said after a moment, "and I must not forget my promise. By the by, I have something in my pocket for you," and drawing up an ottoman he sat down, and unrolling a package, showed me a long stick of "taffy" curiously woven. "Mrs. Mitchell sent over this morning to enquire after the heroine of last night, and, as you missed the best part of the frolic, she sent you this. It liked to have proven a dear 'Sorghum Boiling' both to you and Cousin Rosa."

I smiled, thinking it had indeed proved a dear one to me in one sense of the word. Perhaps he read my thoughts, for he gave me a glance that made me blush, but he forbore to increase my confusion by words, and turned the conversation to something else.

The next hour flew by on rapid wings; for while not uttering one word that could agitate or disturb me, he charmed away pain and weariness by his powers of pleasing and the tender interest which spoke in every tone and glance. When the supper bell summoned him below, he arose and bending down to bid me good-night whispered softly—"Sleep sweetly, little one, remembering that there is one who would sacrifice anything to save you a moment's pain." A tender kiss fell on my forehead, he was gone and I closed my eyes to dream visions of future happiness while I raised my heart in earnest thanksgiving to the Giver of all good who had thus brought me light out of darkness.

When I was able to go down stairs, which was not till the eve of Charley's departure for the army, there was a full explanation between us, and I learned how long and truly I had been loved, though my coldness had left little room for hope that his affection was returned, and had often checked the words which trembled on his lips.

Rosa Harris interrupted this interview. I think she must have guessed how matters stood between us from our happy countenances, for I saw a spasm of pain flit over her face as she pressed her hand to her heart, but the pang, whatever its nature, was soon conquered, or concealed beneath an appearance of gayety which did not fail her during the evening.

The next morning there was a sad parting which each strove to cheer with hopeful anticipations of reunion, and for many days the house seemed very lonely and dull to more than one of us, for Lucy Douglass had taken advantage of Charley's escort to return to her home and Archie who was kept at home by his father's ill health was very desolate; and though Rosa's step was as haughty, and her voice as gay as ever her heavy eyes and pale cheeks spoke of restless nights.

I felt no thrill of triumph in witnessing these signs of distress but from the abundance of my own happiness could afford to pity the pangs which I had once felt myself, and would fain have been friends with her, but the malignant gleam which shot from her brilliant eyes when they rested upon me, told that vindictive feelings rankled beneath which no effort of mine could overcome.

It had been Charley's wish that I should remain at Myrtle Hill, till he was free to claim me; and this invitation his family warmly seconded, but I would not agree to it for I felt that constant occupation would best enable me to bear the great anxiety I must feel for him exposed to all the danger and hardships of a soldier's life; so when my health was fully restored I went back to my city home whose narrow round of duties did not seem irksome now that I had a sweet hope of better days to come, to relieve their tedium.

The days slipped by as time will pass whether we be grave or gay, joyous or miserable, and the period came when "war was no more heard in the land;" the armies were disbanded, and among those whom a kind Providence allowed to return uninjured to their homes was Charley; and one day not long afterward there was a quiet wedding in a city church, and now I am no longer friendless Anna Leigh, but Anna Hilyard rich in the possession of loving hearts and a happy fireside, sit writing at the window of Woodlawn, which is now the home of Charley Hilyard and his happy wife.

Rosa Harris has long since returned to her home in Kentucky—she is still single though rumor says she is soon to marry an old man who has nothing to recommend him but his great wealth. I must ever pity her, believing that she loved my husband as well as she could love any thing but herself.

CHAPTER XVII.

"So endeth the second series of Aunt Quimby's Tales," she said lightly as she closed the book. "You see I have given you as the French would say, *la bonne bouche* for the last, so as to leave a pleasant taste in the mouth; and I hope our journey may end as well as "The Sorghum Boiling, "which you can see is not an autobiography as I am still enjoying single blessedness."

"There is little hope of its having such a romantic termination," said Falstaff with a sigh that Don Quixote declared shook the ambulance, while the sentimental expression he tried to put on was in such ludicrous contrast to his jolly face and form that every body was amused.

"It *is* sad to think that this night will write Finis upon our pleasant trip," said the Historian when the laugh had subsided. "*I*, for one, shall deeply regret that its pleasures are over."

"We will have to console ourselves with the thought that, like most things of the past, it will be moce pleasant in the retrospect than in the reality," said Mrs. Gummidge rather discontentedly.

"I do not see how the *memory* of the past ten days can be any more pleasant than their *realization* has been." said Meg cheerily. *I* thought all of us had enjoyed them thoroughly.

There was a chorus of assents on all sides during which Mrs. Gummidge was heard to murmur something about "bad children," which fortunately escaped the ears of the mothers.

You must excuse Mrs. Gummidge's gloomy face and my black dress;" said Cap, she and I are both in mourning for the *dears* we didn't catch on this hunt. But as it is drawing to a close, and the The Mutual Admiration Society is about to dissolve partnership, I, as the treasurer, have been taking an account of stock and making off a balance sheet. I want you all to see if the items of Profit and Loss are correct;" and opening a sheet of paper she began to read with great gravity:—

"An exhibit of the affairs of The Mutual Admiration Society as taken from their books August 26th, 1868:

LOSSES ON TRIP.

2 Feminine hearts—lost, mislaid or stolen.

1 Vail with an old maid's name on it, which would be gladly exchanged for somebody else's cognomen.

1 Looking glass—broken by the combined looks of the party.

GAINS.

An aching void in the Treasury—filled at starting with $60.

14 Sun-burnt faces and hands.

14 Blistered noses.

7 Tattered dresses and battered sun-bonnets.

1 Royal Buck—shot by Meg—so large she don't know what to do with it.

1 Little *dear*—captured by Manolia, and led captive at will.

"Such being the condition of the finacial department, I would be glad for some one to suggest on which side the balance must be struck, added the accountant."

"If you will add the five other masculine hearts, which you ladies have won, on the side of the *Gains*, I think the balance will fall on that side," said Don Quixote.

"*I* think our title to the last items so doubtful that they had better be placed under the head of *Losses;*" said Aunt Quimby; but the store of pleasant memories we have gathered, is rightfully ours, and I think will counterbalance a few lost hearts; especially as I expect the losers have received others in return."

"Those lost were probably only duplicates, or counterfeits," said the Historian, "for ladies now rarely possess the genuine article."

"No reflection on feminine wares, if you please," said Our Artist, and this was the signal for a wordy war between her and the Historian which lasted till the call was given to stop for dinner, and which ended, as did most of their mimic frays, in an unconditional surrender on the part of the Historian, who declared no defeat could make him any more a slave to her, charms than he already was. A curl of the lip was all the notice she took of his speech, and, declaring she was half dead with fatigue, she sprang out of the ambulance and followed the elders into the large old-fashioned farm house before which they had stopped.

Its inmates, three old maids, were relatives of Lady Montague, and they made the whole party so heartily welcome that the rest in the neat rooms and cool shady yard was duly appreciated by both man and beast.

It was three o'clock in the evening before they again resumed their journey; then by some chance, all the young ladies were scattered in the different vehicles, while the old bachelors of the party, and all the children were settled in the ambulance. This condition of affairs was anything but pleasing to the former, if one might judge from the rueful faces with which they watched these midgets of humanity frisk around them, but no change could be effected before they reached Athens, still about fifteen miles distant, except at the risk of offending the mothers, so nothing was to be done but keep a discreet silence, and try to appear interested in the little folks, who, delighted at their near approach to home, were as full of play as young kittens. So wore away the afternoon hours, and all were delighted when they beheld the sunset rays reflected from the tall spires of Athens.

On the out-skirts of the town, a halt was made to discuss the question whether to spend the night in Athens, or endeavor to reach W——, still seven miles distant. There was a unanimous vote in favor of proceeding, as it promised to be a cloudless night; and it was finally decided to halt the vehicles where they were, feed and rest the tired horses for an hour or two, and finish the remainder of the journey by moon-light.

Under vail of the friendly twilight, which would hide their travel-stained garb, the young people determined to walk down in town; but, on reaching Broad street, nothing would satisfy the gentlemen but that the entire party must adjourn to Flisch's for ice cream.

The temptation to partake of this luxury of civilized life was too great to be resisted even at the risk of meeting some stylish acquaintance, and they were soon seated in the well-lighted saloon, and congratulating themselves that they were the only occupants.

To their palates, so long unregaled by dainties, the ice cream seemed the most delicious ever manufactured, and they lingered over it so long that nine o'clock had struck before they were once more ready to start; then it was Fallstaff's wish that all the young people should collect in the ambulance, so that they might greet their friends at home with music. There was some demurring on the part of the elders, who thought the sleepy children entitled to the best place, but it was overruled, and all proceeded to carry out his wishes with the exception of Cap, who preferred a moonlight ride with Roscius in Falstaff's buggy, which once more led the van.

For several miles after leaving Athens a considerable degree of gloom seemed to hang over the party in the ambulance. Miss Patty and Meg were in the dumps at not being able to continue their ride with the Historian in the double buggy, which they had found so pleasant during the evening. Miss Quimby was occupied by thoughts of her distant home, evoked by the remembrance that of all the party she was the only one who would have no loved ones to welcome her return. Die and Our Artist with their heads close together were exchanging some delightful bits of feminine gossip. Mrs. Gummidge had fallen into another of her low spells, and with her head in Miss Quimby's lap was pretending to sleep at the imminent risk of being precipitated every few minutes on the floor of the vehicle; while the gentlemen were silent, missing Cap's nimble tongue and gleeful laugh; and with all, the thought of the breaking up of the pleasant party added deeper gloom to their musings.

After a time, however, the exceeding beauty and quiet of the night where

> "Pale stars, bright moon, swift cloud made heaven
> so vast
> That earth, left silent by the wind of night,
> Seems shrunken 'neath the gray unmeasured height,"

stole into the depths of their hearts, rounding each jarring note into calm, and they talked in low gentle tones, as of some dear dead thing, of the pleasure of the trip, drew a gentle vail over its discomforts, and planned another for the next summer, till the drivers announced that they were nearly at home. Then all the other vehicles fell back and arranged themselves behind the ambulance, and in this order approached, as quietly as possible, the village, where not a single light was to be seen, as it was near twelve o'clock Reaching the head of the principal street, the choir began the chorus of "Happy Greeting;" and as the procession moved slowly down the street, the horses feet keeping time to the music, the raising of windows, and flickering of lights, told that the village was astir, and here and there from the different homes eager feet ran out to welcome the travelers, while joyful greetings, hurried enquiries, and all the hubbub of arrival resounded on every side. But the merriment was soon hushed by the news that during their absence death had been at work even in that scant population, and at one of the principal houses of the village even now the corpse of one who had been the pride and hope of the household by startling burial. The grim Monster never seems so terrible as when his ghastly presence breaks upon some time of careless mirth, and perhaps nothing could have so thoroughly sobered and brought down our party of tourists to the realities of life as the funeral services which they all attended the next day.

A few days after there was a general breaking up of the merry band, most of whom had only collected in W—— for a summer holiday, of which the trip to the mountains was only one of its many amusements; and now that two years have passed, the circle is so widely severed that there is no hope of ever reuniting its broken links. Some have concluded to continue fellow travelers through life. Of those married Mandia and Iola perhaps think that they have realized their romantic visions in the choice of a companion, while Mrs. Gummidge believes that she she has at length found a faithful Pegotty, and the troubles of "the lone lorn creetur are ended in the haven of matrimony. Several, among then the Historian and Cap, are still monuments of single blesseedness and likely to remain so. Two are far away in a distan State, striving to make themselves a home among strangers, yet still oft sighing for the music of familiar voices, and

> "Alas that thus decay
> Should claim from love a part."

the bodies of Falstaff and Miss Page, the dearest and b[illegible] of that pleasant company, sleep their last long sleep in [illegible] village church-yard, and we hope their spirits are no[illegible] beying upon the Delectable Mountains, or reposing amo[illegible] rich fields and flowing fountains of the land of Beulah; [illegible] we their late fellow travelers, yet linger in the Valley of [illegible] miliation, waiting the command to enter the Enchanted La[illegible] and rest from the toils of the way.

THE END.